## THE GRACIOUS TABLE
## SOUPS BY CAROL

# *100 Gluten Free Soups*

On the *front cover*, top to bottom:
    *Orange Carrot Soup*
    *Yellow and Green Split Pea Soup*
    *Mulligatawny*

On the *back cover*, top to bottom:
    *Cream of Cauliflower Soup*
    *Ginger Broccoli Soup*
    *Orange Turnip Soup*

Copyright © CarTan 2009

ISBN 978-0-9696738-1-1

All rights reserved.

No part of this book may be reproduced in any form, by photocopy, microfilm, xerography, or any other means, or incorporated into any retrieval system, electronic or mechanical, without the written permission of the copyright owner.

**Publisher:** CarTan, Montreal, Canada
**Photography:** Carol Tansey
**Layout Design:** Jacqui Dawson

# CONTENTS

ACKNOWLEDGEMENTS .................................................. v

INTRODUCTION ....................................................... vii

## GLUTEN FREE SOUPS

**CHILLED SOUPS** .................................................... 1

**CREAM SOUPS**

*WITHOUT MEAT* ............................................. 15

*WITH MEAT* ................................................ 33

**FISH CHOWDER** ................................................... 39

**LENTILS, CHICK PEAS, BEANS, SPLIT PEAS** ........................ 47

**VEGETABLE SOUPS**

*WITHOUT MEAT* ............................................. 67

*WITH MEAT* ................................................ 83

**SOUP STOCK** ..................................................... 109

INDEX ............................................................. 116

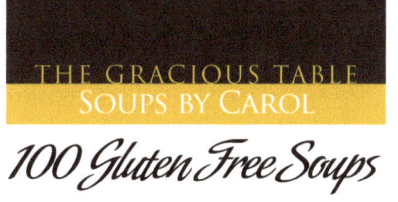

# ACKNOWLEDGEMENTS

I want to thank the tasters – Muriel Johnson, Dianne Belliveau and my sister, Charlotte Tansey, who were the main tasters. Their comments were always helpful and appreciated. Each has her favourite: Muriel – Sweet Potato Soup, Dianne – Pumpkin Soup, Charlotte – French Onion Soup.

There are those who helped to refresh my computer knowledge when I lost it from having several strokes and losing some memory for a certain period of time. They are – Cathy Tansey, her husband, Jean Charbonneau, Ray Cassell, Cynthia Cockburn and Ivy Marie Gumboc. Ivy was most helpful with the finishing stages of the book.

In putting this book together – there were many others – from the Neurologist (who was delighted that I was back on the computer and doing something worthwhile with it) and the Internal Medicine Specialist (who was just very surprised to see me). In the previous and present residences there are health care workers who have given me kind care and encouragement, such as the evening nurse, Myon, in the first facility (who tried to make me appreciate what I could do – instead of what I could not do) and Tess (who brought me a copy book so that I might learn to write again, and so many other kindnesses) and Edna and Hilda here, and Ana.

Especially I say thank you to Lucille (who found a piece of Cheesecake for me in one of my darkest moments), to Lorraine (who supplied the green on the cover of the book and for her suggestion in placing the photos throughout the book), Janessa (who brought me Quebec strawberries and a mango), Pauline and Beverly (who bring me sandwiches in the evening), and Eric (who is always kind to me), Josée (who encourages me to be as mobile as possible), and so many others who make my life and work possible. Thank you all.

Appreciation goes to Patricia Tansey for proof reading the entire manuscript 3 times.

# INTRODUCTION

This book is prepared for those people who must be Gluten Free in their food choices. However, there is no reason why the general public can't also use and enjoy these soup recipes. I serve them to family and friends and they all enjoy them and come back for more.

The non Gluten Free people may not be familiar with the different kinds of flour used – any of which can be obtained at a health food store – OR – regular all purpose flour may be substituted for non Gluten Free people.

But for those who must be Gluten Free there is great variety and delicious taste with really no feeling of denial or limitation. The non Gluten Free people might just enjoy the taste of all the varieties of flour used.

The Gluten Free people should remember that all seasonings they use must be checked out to be Gluten Free. Many manufacturers will send a copy of their Gluten Free products to you if you just give them a phone call. Many have a phone number for customer service on their products and are most agreeable and helpful.

### Gluten Free flour mix for thickening

| | | |
|---|---|---|
| 1 cup | white/brown rice flour | 250 g |
| 5 Tablespoons | potato starch flour | 75 g |
| 2 1/2 Tablespoons | tapioca flour | 37 g |

Mix the 3 Gluten Free flours. Save in freezer and use when called for in different recipes.

For those who must be Gluten Free you should check with your dietitian or physician.

# CHILLED SOUPS

CHILLED CINNAMON APPLE SOUP
CHILLED BANANA SOUP
BORSCHT
CHILLED SOUR CHERRY SOUP
CHILLED STRAWBERRY SOUP

(5 pictures, page 2)

CHILLED PEACH SOUP
CHILLED CREAM OF TURNIP SOUP
CHILLED CUCUMBER SOUP
CHILLED SWEET MYSTERY
CHILLED CANTALOUPE SOUP

(5 pictures, page 6)

CHILLED PINEAPPLE SOUP
CHILLED AVOCADO GRAPEFRUIT SOUP
CHILLED PEA SOUP WITH MINT
CHILLED SWEET MEDLEY
GAZPACHO

(5 pictures, page 11)

1. Chilled Cinnamon Apple Soup
2. Chilled Banana Soup
3. Borscht
4. Chilled Sour Cherry Soup
5. Chilled Strawberry Soup

## Chilled Cinnamon Apple Soup

| 6 | apples, *peeled and chopped* | 6 |
| 1 cup | grapefruit juice | 250 mL |
| 1 1/4 cups | plain yogurt | 310 mL |
| 2/3 cup | maple syrup | 166 mL |
| 1/2 teaspoon | cinnamon | 2 mL |

- Pour grapefruit juice into a medium size bowl. As you peel and chop apples, drop them into grapefruit juice and stir to coat the apples.
- Place apples and grapefruit juice in small amounts into the blender, operate on liquefy.
- When all the apples have been liquefied, place in a large bowl and stir in the yogurt, then the maple syrup and cinnamon. Chill for several hours in the refrigerator.
- Serves 4-6

## Chilled Banana Soup

| 3 | bananas, *peeled and sliced* | 3 |
| 1 cup | grapefruit juice | 250 mL |
| 1 1/2 cups | plain yogurt | 375 mL |
| 5 Tablespoons | maple syrup | 75 mL |
| 1/4 teaspoon | cinnamon | 1 mL |

- Liquefy bananas mixed with grapefruit juice in blender, pour into large bowl.
- Stir in yogurt, maple syrup and cinnamon.
- Chill for several hours in refrigerator.
- Serves 4-6

## Borscht

| | | |
|---|---|---|
| 6 medium | fresh beets | 6 medium |
| 5 1/4 cups | cold water | 1.3 L |
| 3 Tablespoons | fresh lemon juice | 45 mL |
| 1/3 cup | maple syrup | 75 mL |
| 1/2 teaspoon | salt | 2 mL |
| 1/2 cup | sour cream *(optional)* | 125 mL |

- Beets are more easily skinned when cooked. So wash beets, cut top and bottom off, cut in halves or quarters and cook beets with skins on – in just enough water to cover them – until tender, about 1 1/2 hours. Discard water and peel skins from beets.
- Liquefy beets in blender and place in stockpot. *(You really need a blender for this soup – not just a food processor – to get the beets liquefied, not just blended.)*
- Add water, lemon juice, maple syrup and salt. Bring to boil, reduce heat, cover, simmer for 10 minutes. Chill and serve cold – either plain or with a dollop of sour cream.
- Serves 6

*Borscht is so good – of course you have to like beets. The lemon juice adds a real zing to it and the maple syrup rounds it out. Try it and see if you can come to terms with it.*

## Chilled Sour Cherry Soup

| 2 cups | sour cherry juice | 500 mL |
| --- | --- | --- |
| 1/4 cup | sugar | 60 mL |
| 1/4 teaspoon | cinnamon | 1 mL |
| 3 Tablespoons | cold water | 45 mL |
| 5 teaspoons | arrowroot flour | 25 mL |
| 1/4 cup | red wine | 60 mL |
| 1/2 cup | 35% cream | 125 mL |

- Place sour cherry juice, sugar, cinnamon in saucepan. Bring to boil, reduce heat, simmer for 5 minutes.
- In separate dish, stir 3 tablespoons (45 mL) water into arrowroot flour, add a little of the hot soup to it, then add this to soup in saucepan. Stir and continue to simmer for another 5 minutes. Remove from heat and chill.
- When thoroughly chilled and just before serving, add red wine and cream.
- Serves 2-3

## Chilled Strawberry Soup

| 20 | strawberries, *hulled and washed* | 20 |
| --- | --- | --- |
| 1 cup | grapefruit juice | 250 mL |
| 1/2 cup | strawberry jam | 125 mL |
| 1 cup | plain yogurt | 250 mL |
| 1 Tablespoon | maple syrup | 15 mL |
| pinch | cinnamon | pinch |

- Place small amounts of strawberries, grapefruit juice and strawberry jam in blender, operate on liquefy. When these have been liquefied, place in a large bowl, stir in the yogurt, then the maple syrup and cinnamon.
- Chill for several hours in the refrigerator.
- Serves 4

THE GRACIOUS TABLE: SOUPS BY CAROL

1. CHILLED PEACH SOUP
2. CHILLED CREAM OF TURNIP SOUP
3. CHILLED CUCUMBER SOUP
4. CHILLED SWEET MYSTERY
5. CHILLED CANTALOUPE SOUP

6 / CHILLED SOUPS

## CHILLED CREAM OF TURNIP SOUP

| | | |
|---|---|---|
| 1 large | turnip | 1 large |
| 2 Tablespoons | unsalted butter | 30 mL |
| 2 Tablespoons | gluten free flour mix *(see page vii)* | 30 mL |
| 5 1/2 cups | reserved cooking water/cold water | 1.3 L |
| 3 cups | milk | 750 mL |
| 1 cup | light (10 or 15%) cream | 250 mL |
| 1/2 teaspoon | celery salt | 2 mL |
| 1/4 teaspoon | salt | 1 mL |
| 1/2 teaspoon | dried ginger | 2 mL |
| 1 Tablespoon | sugar | 15 mL |
| pinch | cayenne | pinch |

- Peel, cut and cook turnip in water until tender or cook in pressure cooker for 8 minutes. Reserve cooking water. Blend turnip in food processor or blender. Set aside.
- Over medium heat – melt butter, stir in flour, gradually add water, and all other ingredients, including blended turnip, stirring constantly. Bring to boil. Reduce heat, simmer for 5-7 minutes. Cool and refrigerate overnight. Serve chilled.
- Serves 8-10

## CHILLED PEACH SOUP

| | | |
|---|---|---|
| 12 | peaches, *peeled* | 12 |
| 1 small | honey dew melon, *peeled* | 1 small |
| 1 cup | grapefruit juice | 250 mL |
| 1 cup | plain yogurt | 250 mL |
| 3 Tablespoons | maple syrup | 45 mL |
| 1 Tablespoon | ground cinnamon | 15 mL |
| 1 Tablespoon | sugar | 15 mL |

- Liquefy in blender: peaches with grapefruit juice, honey dew melon with yogurt, collect in mixing bowl. Stir together, then stir in maple syrup. Chill in refrigerator for several hours.
- Separately, stir together cinnamon and sugar, and store in a spice shaker. When serving, either shake a little of the cinnamon and sugar on the top of each or pass the shaker around.
- Serves 6

## Chilled Cucumber Soup

| | | |
|---|---|---|
| 2 medium | cucumbers | 2 medium |
| 1 medium | onion | 1 medium |
| 2 1/2 cups | gluten free chicken stock | 625 mL |
| 1 cup | water | 250 mL |
| juice of 1/2 | lemon | juice of 1/2 |
| 1/2 teaspoon | salt | 2 mL |
| pinch | lemon pepper | pinch |
| 3 Tablespoons | white wine | 45 mL |
| 1 Tablespoon | maple syrup | 15 mL |
| 1/2 cup | sour cream | 125 mL |

- Peel cucumbers. Cut in half lengthwise and with a spoon scrape out seeds. Chop cucumbers into small pieces. Peel and chop onion into small pieces.
- Place in saucepan: cucumbers, onion, chicken stock, water, lemon juice, salt. Bring to boil, reduce heat, cover, simmer for 30 minutes.
- Remove from heat, stir in lemon pepper, white wine and maple syrup.
- Chill and serve with a dollop of sour cream.
- Serves 4

*Cucumbers give a lovely fresh taste to a summer soup with a shot of lemon juice and lemon pepper. With a dollop of sour cream – delicious.*

## CHILLED SWEET MYSTERY

| | | |
|---|---|---|
| 8-9 inches | pork bones *(chopped in at least 3 pieces)* | 20-22 cm |
| 8 cups | water | 2 L |
| 1 1/4 teaspoons | salt | 6 mL |
| 1 Tablespoon | apple cider vinegar | 15 mL |
| 2 | bay leaves | 2 |
| | | |
| 1 | leek, *chopped* | 1 |
| 1 large | sweet potato, *peeled and diced* | 1 large |
| 1/2 | English cucumber, *peeled and diced* | 1/2 |
| 1/3 | red pepper, *peeled and chopped* | 1/3 |
| 1/3 | green pepper, *peeled and chopped* | 1/3 |
| 1/3 | yellow pepper, *peeled and chopped* | 1/3 |
| juice of 1 | orange | juice of 1 |
| 1 teaspoon | dried ginger | 5 mL |
| 1/2 teaspoon | cinnamon | 2 mL |
| 1/4 teaspoon | celery salt | 1 mL |
| pinch | cayenne | pinch |
| pinch | garlic powder | pinch |
| 2 Tablespoons | maple syrup | 30 mL |

- Place in stockpot: pork bones, water, salt, apple cider vinegar, bay leaves. Bring to the boil, reduce heat, cover, simmer for 1 hour.
- Remove bones and 2 bay leaves. Strain for any small pieces of bone. Return any bits of meat to the soup. *(If there was much fat on the bones, at this point you might want to set bowl of soup stock in refrigerator overnight, letting fat settle to top, take fat off next day and continue with soup. However, if there was almost no fat, proceed with recipe.)*
- Place soup stock and all remaining ingredients in stockpot, bring to boil, reduce heat, cover, simmer for 7-8 minutes.
- Blend either in food processor or with hand blender. Chill for several hours in refrigerator before serving.
- Serves 6-8

## Chilled Cantaloupe Soup

| | | |
|---|---|---|
| 1 very large | cantaloupe | 1 very large |
| 2 | apples | 2 |
| 2/3 cup | grapefruit juice | 166 mL |
| 1 cup | plain yogurt | 250 mL |
| 2 Tablespoons | maple syrup | 30 mL |
| 1/8 teaspoon | cinnamon | 0.5 mL |

- Skin the cantaloupe, discard skin and seeds. Chop the pulp into pieces and process at liquefy in the blender.
- When the apples are peeled and sliced, immerse the slices in the grapefruit juice, then liquefy in the blender – with the grapefruit juice. Stir all the ingredients together in a mixing bowl.
- Chill in the refrigerator for several hours before serving.
- Serves 6

## Chilled Pineapple Soup

| | | |
|---|---|---|
| 1 whole | pineapple | 1 whole |
| 1/2 cup | grapefruit juice | 125 mL |
| 1 cup | plain yogurt | 250 mL |
| 1/2 cup | maple syrup | 125 mL |
| 1/4 teaspoon | cinnamon | 1 mL |
| 1/8 teaspoon | dried ginger | 0.5 mL |

- Trim pineapple by cutting off top and bottom, removing all skin. Cut pineapple down the middle and remove core. Slice fruit.
- Liquefy the fruit in the blender in small amounts and place in a bowl.
- Stir in grapefruit juice, yogurt, maple syrup, cinnamon, ginger.
- Chill for several hours in the refrigerator.
- Serves 4-6

*100 Gluten Free Soups*

1. Chilled Pineapple Soup
2. Chilled Avocado Grapefruit Soup
3. Chilled Pea Soup with Mint
4. Chilled Sweet Medley
5. Gazpacho

## Chilled Pea Soup with Mint

| | | |
|---|---|---|
| 2 cups | frozen small peas | 500 mL |
| 1 | leek, *trimmed and chopped* | 1 |
| 3 1/2 cups | pork stock *(see page 112)* | 875 mL |
| 1/2 teaspoon | salt | 2 mL |
| 1/2 teaspoon | crushed dried mint | 2 mL |
| 2 Tablespoons | arrowroot flour | 30 mL |
| 1/2 cup | water | 125 mL |
| 4 Tablespoons | 35% cream | 60 mL |

- Place in stockpot: frozen peas, chopped leek, pork stock, salt, mint. Bring to boil, reduce heat, cover, simmer for 5 minutes.
- In a separate dish: stir flour and water together, add a little of the hot soup to it, then add this to soup. Continue to simmer for another 5 minutes.
- Blend with hand blender, then strain – using a spoon to extract all the juice possible from the peas left in strainer. Discard pulp. Stir cream into soup, cool, chill in refrigerator for several hours.
- *Variation:* equally delicious served as a hot soup.
- Serves 4

## Chilled Avocado Grapefruit Soup

| | | |
|---|---|---|
| 2 | avocados | 2 |
| 1 cup | grapefruit juice | 250 mL |
| 1 cup | plain yogurt | 250 mL |
| 1 1/2 cups | cold water | 375 mL |
| 2 Tablespoons | maple syrup | 30 mL |
| 1/4 teaspoon | salt | 1 mL |

- Cut avocados open, scrape flesh out of skin, place in blender and liquefy, adding grapefruit juice first, then yogurt. Turn out into mixing bowl, stir in water, maple syrup and salt.
- Chill in refrigerator for several hours.
- Serves 4

## CHILLED SWEET MEDLEY

| | | |
|---|---|---|
| 2 large | apples, *peeled and chopped* | 2 large |
| 2 1/2 | bananas, *peeled and sliced* | 2 1/2 |
| 1/4 | cantaloupe, *skinned and chopped* | 1/4 |
| 1/2 | juice of 1/2 lemon | 1/2 |
| 1 cup | grapefruit juice | 250 mL |
| 1 cup | plain yogurt | 250 mL |
| 1/2 cup | maple syrup | 125 mL |
| 3/4 teaspoon | cinnamon | 3 mL |

- Prepare fruits and immerse them in lemon juice and grapefruit juice mixed.
- Liquefy fruits, in small amounts, in blender, with the juice. Place in large bowl. Stir in yogurt, maple syrup and cinnamon. Chill for several hours in the refrigerator.
- Serves 4-6

## GAZPACHO

| | | |
|---|---|---|
| 1 | cucumber, *peeled, seeded and diced* | 1 |
| 1 clove | garlic, *peeled and chopped* | 1 clove |
| 2 Tablespoons | olive oil | 30 mL |
| 1 | green pepper, *peeled, seeded and diced* | 1 |
| 3 | tomatoes, *peeled and diced* | 3 |
| 1 1/4 cups | tinned ground tomatoes | 310 mL |
| 1 1/4 cups | cold water | 310 mL |
| 2 Tablespoons | apple cider vinegar | 30 mL |
| 2 Tablespoons | balsamic vinegar | 30 mL |
| 1 Tablespoon | sugar | 15 mL |
| 1 teaspoon | salt | 5 mL |
| pinch | cayenne | pinch |
| pinch | white pepper | pinch |

- For those people who are unable to tolerate raw cucumber or raw garlic, no need to deny yourselves the delights of Gazpacho, just fry cucumber and garlic in olive oil for 5-7 minutes until coated with the oil and opaque. Place in large mixing bowl. Stir in remainder of ingredients. Chill in refrigerator for several hours. Serve cold.
- This soup does not freeze well. It is best eaten within a day or two of preparation to experience the delicious taste and consistency.
- Serves 6

# CREAM SOUPS WITHOUT MEAT

*CREAM OF ASPARAGUS SOUP*

*CREAM OF CAULIFLOWER SOUP*

*CELERY SOUP WITH GINGER*

*CELERY SOUP WITH TARRAGON*

*CELERY SOUP WITH ONION*

*(5 pictures, page 16)*

*CORN CHOWDER*

*CREAM OF CORN SOUP*

*LEEK AND POTATO SOUP*

*VICHYSSOISE*

*CREAM OF MUSHROOM SOUP*

*(5 pictures, page 21)*

*PUMPKIN SOUP*

*GINGER SQUASH SOUP*

*SWEET POTATO SOUP*

*STRAWBERRY GINGER SOUP*

*(4 pictures, page 25)*

*CREAMY GREEN VEGETABLE SOUP*

*CREAM OF TOMATO SOUP*

*WATERCRESS SOUP*

*(3 pictures, page 30)*

THE GRACIOUS TABLE: SOUPS BY CAROL

1. **Cream of Asparagus Soup**
2. **Cream of Cauliflower Soup**
3. **Celery Soup with Ginger**
4. **Celery Soup with Onion**
5. **Celery Soup with Tarragon**

16 / Cream Soups without Meat

## CREAM OF ASPARAGUS SOUP

| 45 | asparagus *(some thin, some thick)* | 45 |
|---|---|---|
| 5 cups | cold water | 1.2 L |
| 2 Tablespoons | olive oil | 30 mL |
| 3 Tablespoons | brown rice flour mix | 45 mL |
| 2 1/2 cups | milk | 625 mL |
| 1/4 teaspoon | celery salt | 1 mL |
| 1/2 teaspoon | fine herbs *(mixture of parsley, chives, tarragon)* | 2 mL |
| 1/2 teaspoon | salt | 2 mL |
| 1/8 teaspoon | cayenne | 0.5 mL |

- Break off and dispose of hard ends of asparagus. Cook the asparagus in 5 cups water (1.2 L) until just tender. Save a few tips for garnishing. Blend asparagus with cooking water. Set aside.

- Place olive oil in stockpot, stir in flour mix. While continuing to stir, add blended asparagus, then add milk. Stir in seasonings. Bring to boil, reduce heat, simmer for 7 minutes. Serve garnished with tips of asparagus.

- Serves 6

*Asparagus Soup brings very mixed memories to mind. My Father was suffering both brain damage and terrible physical injuries from a traffic accident. A very good friend of ours, Mary Savor, would often come to our home with fresh asparagus – just when they were fresh in early Spring. We came to love asparagus because it was so very kind of her.*

## Cream of Cauliflower Soup

| | | |
|---|---|---|
| 1 medium | cauliflower | 1 medium |
| 1 cup | cooking water | 250 mL |
| 3 Tablespoons | butter or olive oil | 45 mL |
| 3 Tablespoons | gluten free flour mix *(see page vii)* | 45 mL |
| 3 1/2 cups | cold water | 875 mL |
| 1 cup | milk | 250 mL |
| 1 large clove | garlic, *crushed* | 1 large clove |
| 1/2 teaspoon | celery salt | 2 mL |
| 1/2 teaspoon | dried ginger | 2 mL |
| 1/2 teaspoon | salt | 2 mL |
| pinch | white pepper | pinch |
| pinch | cayenne | pinch |
| 2 Tablespoons | maple syrup | 30 mL |
| 1/2 cup | grated cheddar cheese | 125 mL |

- Cook cauliflower until almost tender – about 7-8 minutes. Cool slightly. Blend with 1 cup (250 mL) cooking water. Set aside.
- Place butter or olive oil in stockpot, over medium heat. Stir in flour, add water gradually, stirring constantly. Add blended cauliflower, stir in milk and seasonings, bring to boil. Reduce heat, cover, simmer for 5-7 minutes.
- Serve with grated cheddar cheese sprinkled on top.
- Serves 5-6  *(Picture on back cover)*

*Cauliflower Soup is just so delicious with seasonings and grated cheddar cheese – that I even put it on the back cover. It has a very delicate flavour.*

## CELERY SOUP WITH GINGER

| | | |
|---|---|---|
| 8 cups | chopped celery | 1.8 L |
| 4 cups | water | 1 L |
| 1 1/4 teaspoons | salt | 6 mL |
| 5 Tablespoons | brown rice flour mix | 75 mL |
| 1 cup | water | 250 mL |
| 2 cups | milk | 500 mL |
| 1 teaspoon | dried ginger | 5 mL |
| 4 Tablespoons | maple syrup | 60 mL |

- Place celery, water, salt in stockpot. Bring to boil, reduce heat. Cover and simmer for 15 minutes. Remove from heat. Blend with hand blender.
- In a small bowl, mix flour with 1 cup water (250 mL) and add to celery soup – first adding a little of the hot mixture to it. Stir and add milk, maple syrup and ginger. Bring to boil, reduce heat, cover and simmer for 5-7 minutes. Blend with hand blender, strain and reheat before serving. Serve with grated cheddar cheese (optional).
- Serves 8

## CELERY SOUP WITH TARRAGON

| | | |
|---|---|---|
| 5 cups | chopped celery | 1.2 L |
| 3 cups | water | 750 mL |
| 1 teaspoon | salt | 5 mL |
| 4 Tablespoons | brown rice flour mix | 60 mL |
| 1/2 cup | water | 125 mL |
| 2 cups | milk | 500 mL |
| 1 Tablespoon | maple syrup | 15 mL |
| 1/2 teaspoon | dried tarragon leaves | 2 mL |

- Place celery, water, salt in stockpot. Bring to boil, reduce heat, cover, simmer for 15 minutes. In a small saucepan mix flour with 1/2 cup (125 mL) water and add to celery soup – first adding a little of the hot mixture to it. Stir and add milk, maple syrup and tarragon. Bring to boil, reduce heat, cover, simmer for 5-7 minutes. Blend with hand blender, strain and reheat before serving.
- Serves 5

## Celery Soup with Onion

| | | |
|---|---|---|
| 2 Tablespoons | olive oil | 30 mL |
| 3 cups | chopped celery | 750 mL |
| 1 | chopped onion | 1 |
| 3 cups | cold water | 750 mL |
| 1 teaspoon | salt | 5 mL |
| | | |
| 1/2 cup | water | 125 mL |
| 2 Tablespoons | tapioca flour | 30 mL |
| | | |
| 3 cups | milk | 750 mL |
| 1 teaspoon | dried ginger | 5 mL |
| 1/2 Tablespoon | sugar | 7 mL |
| 1 teaspoon | celery salt | 5 mL |
| pinch | white pepper | pinch |
| pinch | cayenne | pinch |
| 1 Tablespoon | maple syrup | 15 mL |
| | | |
| 1 cup | grated cheddar cheese *(optional)* | 250 mL |

- Place olive oil in stockpot, add celery and onion and cook over medium heat for 5 minutes, stirring occasionally. Add water and salt, bring to boil, reduce heat, cover and simmer for 15-20 minutes until celery and onion are tender. Remove from heat, strain for celery strings.
- In a small bowl, mix flour with 1/2 cup (125 mL) water and add to celery soup – first adding a little of the hot mixture to it.
- Stir and add milk and seasonings. Bring to boil, reduce heat, cover and simmer for 5-7 minutes. Blend with hand blender. Reheat before serving.
- Serve with grated cheddar cheese *(optional)*.
- Serves 7

*100 Gluten Free Soups*

1. Corn Chowder
2. Cream of Corn Soup
3. Leek and Potato Soup
4. Vichyssoise
5. Cream of Mushroom Soup

Cream Soups without Meat / 21

## Corn Chowder

| | | |
|---|---|---|
| 4 | corn on the cob | 4 |
| 4 Tablespoons | butter | 60 mL |
| 1 medium | onion, *peeled and chopped* | 1 medium |
| 2 medium | potatoes, *peeled and diced* | 2 medium |
| 1 teaspoon | salt | 5 mL |
| 2 cups | reserved cooking water | 500 mL |
| 1 cup | milk | 250 mL |
| 1/2 cup | 10% cream | 125 mL |
| pinch | white pepper | pinch |

- Peel the husks off the corn and drop the corn into boiling water, cook for 10 minutes. Reserve the cooking water. Scrape the corn off the cobs. Set corn kernels aside.

- Place butter in saucepan, add chopped onion, simmer for 3-4 minutes, then add diced potatoes, salt and reserved cooking water. Bring to boil, reduce heat, cover, simmer for 15 minutes. Mash with potato masher. Add corn kernels, milk, cream, white pepper. Stir, bring to boil, reduce heat, cover and simmer for 5 minutes.

- Serves 4

## Cream of Corn Soup

| | | |
|---|---|---|
| 8 | corn on the cob | 8 |
| 4 Tablespoons | butter | 60 mL |
| 1/2 teaspoon | salt | 2 mL |
| 3 cups | reserved cooking water | 750 mL |
| 1/2 cup | corn soup | 125 mL |
| 3 Tablespoons | white rice flour mix | 45 mL |
| 1 cup | 10% cream | 250 mL |
| 1 cup | milk | 250 mL |
| pinch | white pepper | pinch |

- Peel husks off corn and drop it into boiling salted water. Cook for 10 minutes. Reserve 3 cups (750 mL) cooking water. Scrape corn off cobs, blend corn in food processor or blender. Fry blended corn in butter for 3-4 minutes, add salt and reserved cooking water, bring to boil, reduce heat, simmer for 5 minutes.

- In a separate dish, stir 1/2 cup (125 mL) corn soup into flour, then pour mixture gradually back into the soup, stirring constantly so that lumps do not form. Continue to simmer soup for 3-4 minutes while adding cream, milk, white pepper.

- Serves 4

## Leek and Potato Soup

| | | |
|---|---|---|
| 4 large | potatoes | 4 large |
| 3 large | leeks | 3 large |
| 5 cups | cold water | 1.2 L |
| 1 teaspoon | salt | 5 mL |
| 1/4 teaspoon | celery salt | 1 mL |
| 1 teaspoon | lemon juice | 5 mL |

- Peel potatoes, cut in chunks.
- Trim leeks – leaving small amount of green above the white base, wash carefully, slice across. Place potatoes, leeks and salt in cold water – bring to boil, reduce heat, simmer for 15 minutes. Remove from heat. Blend with hand blender. Strain for strings of leeks.
- Add lemon juice, celery salt. Bring to boil, reduce heat, cover, simmer for 5 minutes.
- Serve hot.
- Serves 6

## Vichyssoise

Same as above – but after it has finished cooking and has been run through sieve, stir in slowly:

| | | |
|---|---|---|
| 1 cup | 15% cream | 250 mL |

- Chill in refrigerator and serve cold.
- Serves 6

## Cream of Mushroom Soup

| | | |
|---|---|---|
| 3 Tablespoons | butter | 45 mL |
| 4 Tablespoons | gluten free brown rice flour mix | 60 mL |
| 1 cup | cold water | 250 mL |
| 3 cups | milk | 750 mL |
| 3 cups | finely chopped mushrooms, *white and shiitake mixed* | 750 mL |
| 1 teaspoon | salt | 5 mL |
| 1/2 teaspoon | celery seed | 2 mL |
| 1/4 teaspoon | dill seed | 1 mL |
| 1/2 teaspoon | dried basil | 2 mL |
| 1/8 teaspoon | black pepper | 0.5 mL |
| 1/8 teaspoon | cayenne | 0.5 mL |
| 1/2 teaspoon | dried minced onion | 2 mL |

- Melt butter in stockpot, stir in mushrooms, cook gently for 5 minutes, add flour, then water and milk slowly, stirring to smooth consistency.
- Add all seasonings, bring to boil, reduce heat and simmer for 5 minutes.
- Serves 4

*The best Mushroom Soup I ever had was in Dublin, Ireland. We arrived at the hotel around 1 pm from the airport. We had lunch immediately – Mushroom Soup followed by Salmon Steak – it was gorgeous.*

*I hope the reader will make some good memories of my Mushroom Soup.*

*100 Gluten Free Soups*

1. Pumpkin Soup
2. Ginger Squash Soup
3. Sweet Potato Soup
4. Strawberry Ginger Soup

Cream Soups without Meat / 25

## Pumpkin Soup

| | | |
|---|---|---|
| 3 1/4 cups | tinned pumpkin | 796 mL |
| 6 cups | cold water | 1.3 L |
| 2 1/4 cups | milk | 560 mL |
| 1 1/4 teaspoons | salt | 6 mL |
| 1/4 teaspoon | black pepper | 1 mL |
| 3 Tablespoons | sugar | 45 mL |
| 3/4 teaspoon | dried cinnamon | 3 mL |
| 3/4 teaspoon | dried ginger | 3 mL |
| 1/3 cup | maple syrup | 75 mL |
| 1 cup | orange juice | 250 mL |
| 1/4 cup | cold water | 60 mL |
| 1 Tablespoon | gluten free brown rice flour mix | 15 mL |
| 1/3 cup | 10% cream | 75 mL |

- Place pumpkin pulp, water, milk, seasonings and maple syrup in stockpot, stir, bring to boil, reduce heat, stir in orange juice slowly, cover and simmer for 5 minutes.

- In a separate dish – stir 1/4 cup (60 mL) cold water into flour mix, add to soup and stir, first adding a little of the hot soup to it. Continue to simmer, covered, for 7 minutes to cook the flour.

- Remove from heat, slowly stir in cream.

- Serves 10

*Pumpkin is so versatile – it can be used to make soup, cheesecake, pie, cookies, bread, and they are all so gorgeous. I make an excellent Pumpkin Cheesecake – even it can be made gluten free.*

## GINGER SQUASH SOUP

| | | | |
|---|---|---|---|
| | 2 small | pepper squash | 2 small |
| OR | 1 large | butternut squash | 1 large |
| | 1 cup | orange juice | 250 mL |
| | 1/2 cup | water | 125 mL |
| | 2 Tablespoons | arrowroot flour | 30 mL |
| | 1/4 cup | water | 60 mL |
| | 4 cups | water | 1 L |
| | 1 1/4 teaspoons | dried ginger | 6 mL |
| | 1/2 teaspoon | dried cinnamon | 2 mL |
| | 1 teaspoon | salt | 5 mL |
| | 3 Tablespoons | maple syrup | 45 mL |
| | pinch | white pepper | pinch |
| | pinch | cayenne | pinch |
| | 1 cup | 10% cream | 250 mL |

- Place squash in a stockpot, cover with water, cook until soft – about 1 1/4 hours. Cut squash in half, discard seeds, scoop out squash. This will yield 3 cups (750 mL) of cooked squash.
- Blend the cooked squash with 1 cup (250 mL) orange juice and 1/2 cup (125 mL) water. Place blended squash in stockpot.
- In a separate dish, mix arrowroot flour and 1/4 cup (60 mL) water. Set aside.
- Add to stockpot: 4 cups (1 L) water, dried ginger, cinnamon, salt, maple syrup, white pepper, cayenne. Stir, bring to the boil, reduce heat and simmer for 5 minutes.
- Stir into soup in stockpot the arrowroot flour and water, first adding a little of the hot mixture to it. Continue to simmer for 5 minutes.
- Remove from heat, stir in cream slowly.
- Serves 6

## Sweet Potato Soup

| | | |
|---|---|---|
| 2 | large sweet potatoes | 2 |
| 1 | fennel bulb | 1 |
| 6 cups | water | 1.5 L |
| 1 teaspoon | salt | 5 mL |
| 3 Tablespoons | arrowroot flour | 45 mL |
| 1 1/2 cups | milk | 375 mL |
| 1/2 cup | maple syrup | 125 mL |
| 1/4 teaspoon | cinnamon | 1 mL |
| 1/2 teaspoon | garlic powder | 2 mL |
| 1/4 teaspoon | dried ginger | 1 mL |
| 1/8 teaspoon | cayenne | 0.5 mL |
| 1/8 teaspoon | white pepper | 0.5 mL |
| 2 teaspoons | apple cider vinegar | 10 mL |
| 1/2 cup | 15% cream | 125 mL |

- Peel and chop sweet potatoes. Trim fennel bulb by removing outer layer and inner core and the stem and greenery on the top – use only the trimmed bulb and chop it.

- Place sweet potatoes, fennel, water and salt in stockpot. Bring to the boil, reduce heat, cover and simmer for 15 minutes or until sweet potato is just cooked. Remove from heat, blend with hand blender.

- In a separate dish – add milk gradually to flour, then add this to the soup – first adding a little of the hot mixture to the flour mixture. Add all seasonings (not the cream yet), return to the boil, reduce heat and simmer, covered, for 10 minutes. Remove from heat, stir in cream.

- Pass soup through a strainer *(in case any strings remain from the fennel)*. Reheat if serving immediately, but do not boil.

- Serves 8

## Strawberry Ginger Soup

| 2 cups | sliced strawberries | 500 mL |
| --- | --- | --- |
| 2 | onions, *peeled and chopped* | 2 |
| 4 | carrots, *peeled and sliced* | 4 |
| 1 | leek, *trimmed and sliced* | 1 |
| 5 cups | water | 1.2 L |
| 1/2 teaspoon | salt | 2 mL |
| 3/4 cup | tinned ground tomatoes | 175 mL |
| 2 1/2 teaspoons | dried ginger | 12 mL |
| 1/2 teaspoon | dried dill weed | 2 mL |
| pinch | white pepper | pinch |
| pinch | cayenne | pinch |
| 1 Tablespoon | sugar | 15 mL |
| 3 Tablespoons | maple syrup | 45 mL |
| 1 cup | 15% cream | 250 mL |

- Place all ingredients – except cream – in large stockpot. Bring to boil, reduce heat, cover, simmer for 25 minutes. Blend with hand blender.
- Stir in cream gradually. Give a quick blend with hand blender if required.
- Serves 6

*This is a nice, smooth, creamy soup with an over taste of strawberry and ginger, yet with onion, carrot and leek for nutritious value. It is kind of a surprise.*

THE GRACIOUS TABLE: SOUPS BY CAROL

1. Creamy Green Vegetable Soup
2. Cream of Tomato Soup
3. Watercress Soup

30 / Cream Soups without Meat

## CREAMY GREEN VEGETABLE SOUP

| | | |
|---|---|---|
| 10 1/2 oz | frozen spinach | 300 g |
| 1 | zucchini, *peeled and sliced* | 1 |
| 1/2 head | broccoli *(flowerets with short stem)* | 1/2 head |
| 5 stalks | celery, *strings removed, chopped* | 5 stalks |
| 5 | green leaves Romaine lettuce | 5 |
| 1/2 | English cucumber, *peeled and chopped* | 1/2 |
| 4 1/2 cups | water | 1 L |
| 1 teaspoon | salt | 5 mL |
| pinch | white pepper | pinch |
| 1/4 teaspoon | garlic powder | 1 mL |
| 2 pinches | cayenne | 2 pinches |
| 1 teaspoon | dried tarragon leaves | 5 mL |
| 1/2 teaspoon | celery salt | 2 mL |
| 1 cup | 35% cream | 250 mL |

- Place all ingredients – except cream – in large stockpot. Bring to boil, reduce heat, cover, simmer for 20 minutes. Blend with hand blender.
- Stir in cream.
- Bring back to simmer for 1 minute – if serving immediately.
- Serves 6

*This is an interesting soup – with so many greens in it – and the seasonings to bring them to life – and cream to enrich them. Of course the cream could be reduced to light cream or milk if there is too much fat in the diet. But it is a delicious soup as is.*

## Cream of Tomato Soup

| | | |
|---|---|---|
| 28 oz tin | ground tomatoes | 796 mL |
| 2 1/2 cups | water | 625 mL |
| 2 1/2 cups | milk | 625 mL |
| 1 Tablespoon | sugar | 15 mL |
| 1/2 teaspoon | dried oregano | 2 mL |
| 1 1/2 teaspoons | dried basil | 7 mL |
| 1/3 teaspoon | salt | 1.5 mL |
| 1 teaspoon | dill weed | 5 mL |
| pinch | cayenne | pinch |
| 1/8 teaspoon | white pepper | 0.5 mL |
| 1/8 teaspoon | dried ginger | 0.5 mL |
| 2 Tablespoons | gluten free flour mix *(see page vii)* | 30 mL |
| 1 Tablespoon | olive oil | 15 mL |
| 1/4 cup | maple syrup | 60 mL |
| 1 cup | 10% cream | 250 mL |

- Place in stockpot – tomatoes, water, milk, sugar and all seasonings. Bring to boil, reduce heat, cover and simmer for 7 minutes.
- In a separate dish, mix flour and olive oil and put in with soup. Blend with hand blender. Continue to simmer for another 7 minutes. Turn heat off, stir in maple syrup and cream.
- Serves 6

## Watercress Soup

| | | |
|---|---|---|
| 3 cups | leeks, *washed and chopped* | 750 mL |
| 3 cups | potatoes, *peeled and chopped* | 750 mL |
| 5 cups | water | 1.2 L |
| 1/2 teaspoon | salt | 2 mL |
| 2 bunches | watercress, *washed and chopped* | 2 bunches |
| 1 cup | 15% cream | 250 mL |

- Place leeks, potatoes, water, salt in stockpot. Bring to boil, reduce heat, cover and simmer for 10-15 minutes until vegetables are nearly done.
- Add watercress, continue to simmer for 5 minutes. Blend with hand blender. Stir in cream while continuing to blend.
- Serves 6

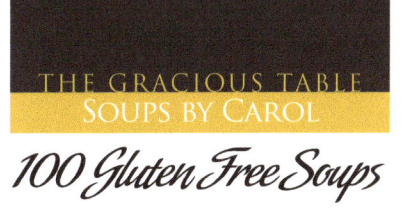

# CREAM SOUPS WITH MEAT

*CREAM OF RUTABAGA SOUP*

*GINGER BROCCOLI SOUP*

*SPINACH SOUP*

*BRUSSEL SPROUTS SOUP*

*CURRIED CARROT SOUP*

(5 pictures, page 34)

# THE GRACIOUS TABLE: SOUPS BY CAROL

1. Cream of Rutabaga Soup
2. Ginger Broccoli Soup
3. Spinach Soup
4. Brussel Sprouts Soup
5. Curried Carrot Soup

34 / Cream Soups with Meat

## Cream of Rutabaga Soup

| | | |
|---|---|---|
| 2 medium | rutabagas | 2 medium |
| 1 cup | reserved cooking water | 250 mL |
| 2 Tablespoons | olive oil | 30 mL |
| 3 Tablespoons | gluten free flour mix *(see page vii)* | 45 mL |
| 6 cups | gluten free chicken stock | 1.4 L |
| 1/4 cup | maple syrup | 60 mL |
| 1/2 cup | milk | 125 mL |
| pinch | cayenne | pinch |
| 1 teaspoon | dried ginger | 5 mL |
| 1 teaspoon | dried dill weed | 5 mL |
| 1/4 teaspoon | paprika | 1 mL |
| 1 cup | 10% cream | 250 mL |

- Cut into chunks and boil the 2 rutabagas. Cool and blend with 1 cup (250 mL) reserved cooking water. Set aside.
- Place olive oil in stockpot over medium heat, add flour and mix. Stir in chicken stock slowly, then add all other ingredients (except cream) – including blended rutabagas. *(If rutabagas are large – add more milk or water to correct consistency.)*
- Stir, bring to boil, reduce heat, cover and simmer for 10 minutes. Remove from heat, give a quick blend with hand blender. Stir in cream. Taste for salt. *(Chicken Stock has salt in it – so soup may not need any.)*
- Serves 8

*Cream of Rutabaga Soup is very nice and almost indistinguishable from Turnip Soup.*

## GINGER BROCCOLI SOUP

| | | |
|---|---|---|
| 1 1/2 heads | broccoli *(flowerets with short stem)* | 1 1/2 heads |
| 6 cups | water | 1.4 L |
| 2 1/2 Tablespoons | gluten free chicken soup base | 37 mL |
| 1 1/4 cups | milk | 310 mL |
| 1/4 cup | gluten free flour mix *(see page vii)* | 60 mL |
| 1/4 cup | cold water | 60 mL |
| 1 teaspoon | celery salt | 5 mL |
| 3/4 teaspoon | dried ginger | 3 mL |
| pinch | white pepper | pinch |
| pinch | cayenne | pinch |

- Add chicken soup base to boiling water, simmer for 3 minutes, add broccoli. Return to boil, reduce heat, cover, simmer for 10 minutes until broccoli is tender. Remove from heat. Blend broccoli with hand blender. Add milk gradually and stir.

- In small bowl, blend flour with cold water and add to soup gradually, first adding a little of hot soup to flour mix, stir. Return to boil, add seasonings. Reduce heat, simmer for 5 minutes. Blend with hand blender – if necessary. Taste for salt.

- **Serves 7** *(Picture on back cover)*

*Ginger Broccoli Soup is a very good simple soup.*

*NOTE: When following any recipe, pay attention to the difference between chicken base and chicken stock. They are similar – but the base is the powder that you add to the water, the stock is the liquid that you use instead.*

## Spinach Soup

| | | |
|---|---|---|
| 8 cups | boiling water | 1.8 L |
| 3 Tablespoons | gluten free chicken soup base | 45 mL |
| 2 Tablespoons | olive oil | 30 mL |
| 2 large | onions, *peeled and chopped* | 2 large |
| 2 pkgs (300 g each) | frozen spinach | 600 g |
| 1/3 cup | uncooked basmati white rice | 75 mL |
| 2 cups | milk | 500 mL |
| 2 cups | water | 500 mL |
| 1 teaspoon | dried basil | 5 mL |
| 1 teaspoon | dried dill weed | 5 mL |
| 2 pinches | white pepper | 2 pinches |
| 2 pinches | cayenne | 2 pinches |
| 1 Tablespoon | sugar | 15 mL |

- Dissolve soup base in boiling water, stir and simmer for 1 minute. *(Do not add salt – as soup base has enough).*
- Add the remainder of the ingredients. Return to boil, reduce heat, cover and simmer for 20 minutes or until spinach is thawed and cooked and rice is cooked. Blend with hand blender.
- Serves 10

*Spinach is one of my favorite soups with basmati white rice. It is so good, and so good for you.*

## Brussel Sprouts Soup

| | | |
|---|---|---|
| 3 cups | water | 750 mL |
| 2 Tablespoons | gluten free chicken soup base | 30 mL |
| 1 pound | brussel sprouts, *trimmed, washed and cut in half* | 500 g |
| 3/4 teaspoon | lemon pepper | 3 mL |
| 1/2 cup | 15% cream | 125 mL |
| 1/2 cup | milk | 125 mL |

- To boiling water, stir in chicken soup base, reduce heat, simmer for 3 minutes. Add brussel sprouts, return to boil, reduce heat, cover, simmer for 10 minutes. Add lemon pepper, cream, milk. Blend with hand blender. Simmer until warm if serving immediately. *(Do not add salt as soup base has enough.)*

- Serves 4

## Curried Carrot Soup

| | | |
|---|---|---|
| 5 1/2 cups | turkey stock *(see page 114)* | 1.3 L |
| 2 cups | water | 500 mL |
| 3 large | carrots, *peeled and grated* | 3 large |
| 3 | apples, *peeled and grated* | 3 |
| 1 1/2 teaspoons | hot curry powder | 7 mL |
| 1 teaspoon | salt | 5 mL |
| 1/2 cup | uncooked basmati rice | 125 mL |
| 1 1/2 cups | orange juice | 375 mL |
| 1/4 cup | water | 60 mL |
| 2 Tablespoons | potato flour | 30 mL |
| 1 cup | milk | 250 mL |

- Place in stockpot: turkey stock, 2 cups (500 mL) water, carrots, apples, curry powder, salt, rice, orange juice. Bring to boil, reduce heat, cover and simmer for 15 minutes.

- In a separate dish – stir 1/4 cup (60 mL) water into potato flour, add to hot mixture – first adding a little of the hot mixture to it. Stir in milk. Simmer for 5 minutes. Blend with hand blender.

- Serves 6

# Fish Chowder

*SEAFOOD DELIGHT*

*TURBOT CHOWDER*

*CLAM CHOWDER*

*SCALLOP CHOWDER*

*(4 pictures, page 40)*

*SHRIMP BISQUE*

*HALIBUT CHOWDER*

*MONTREAL CHOWDER*

*(3 pictures, page 43)*

THE GRACIOUS TABLE: SOUPS BY CAROL

1 Seafood Delight
2 Turbot Chowder
3 Clam Chowder
4 Scallop Chowder

40 / Fish Chowder

## SEAFOOD DELIGHT

| | | |
|---|---|---|
| 2 Tablespoons | olive oil | 30 mL |
| 3 Tablespoons | arrowroot flour | 45 mL |
| 1 | leek, *chopped* | 1 |
| 1 1/2 cups | vegetable stock | 375 mL |
| 1 cup | water | 250 mL |
| 1 cup | frozen peas, *small size* | 250 mL |
| 1 cup | cooked small shrimp | 250 mL |
| 1 cup | cooked crab | 250 mL |
| 2 pinches | cayenne | 2 pinches |
| 1/2 teaspoon | salt | 2 mL |
| 1 cup | 10% cream | 250 mL |
| 1 cup | milk | 250 mL |
| 2 Tablespoons | grated parmesan cheese | 30 mL |

- Place olive oil into stockpot on medium heat, stir in arrowroot flour and chopped leek, cook for 2-3 minutes.
- Add all other ingredients, adding cream, milk and cheese at the last. Bring almost to the boiling point – but do not boil – reduce heat and simmer for 5 minutes.
- Serves 6

## TURBOT CHOWDER

| | | |
|---|---|---|
| 1 Tablespoon | olive oil | 15 mL |
| 1 | leek, *trimmed and sliced* | 1 |
| 2 med/large | potatoes, *peeled, cut in chunks* | 2 med/large |
| 1/2 pound | turbot fillets, *cut in small pieces* | 250 g |
| 2 cups | water | 500 mL |
| 1/2 teaspoon | salt | 2 mL |
| pinch | white pepper | pinch |
| 1 1/2 cups | milk | 375 mL |

- Place olive oil in medium size saucepan, add sliced leek, fry for 3-4 minutes. Add potatoes, fish, water, salt, pepper. Bring to the boil, reduce heat, cover and simmer for 15 minutes. Add milk, simmer for 5 minutes.
- *Variation:* Usually the fish used is haddock or cod.
- Serves 4

## Clam Chowder

| | | |
|---|---|---|
| 4 small/med | potatoes, *peeled and diced* | 4 small/med |
| 2 medium | onions, *peeled and diced* | 2 medium |
| 2 | bay leaves | 2 |
| 3 cups | water | 750 mL |
| 2 Tablespoons | butter | 30 mL |
| 1/4 teaspoon | dried thyme | 1 mL |
| 1/4 teaspoon | salt | 1 mL |
| pinch | white pepper | pinch |
| 1 1/4 cups | tinned whole baby clams with juice | 310 mL |
| 1/2 cup | 15% cream | 125 mL |

- Place in stockpot: potatoes, onions, bay leaves, water. Bring to boil, reduce heat, cover, simmer for 10 minutes. Remove 2 bay leaves. Add: butter, thyme, salt, pepper, baby clams with juice, continue to simmer for 4-5 minutes. Remove from heat, slowly stir in cream and serve.
- Serves 5

## Scallop Chowder

| | | |
|---|---|---|
| 2 large | potatoes, *peeled and diced* | 2 large |
| 2 | onions, *peeled and chopped* | 2 |
| 4 cups | water | 1 L |
| 1 teaspoon | salt | 5 mL |
| pinch | white pepper | pinch |
| 1/2 pound | small scallops | 250 g |
| 2/3 cup | frozen small peas | 150 mL |
| 1/2 teaspoon | dried marjoram leaves | 2 mL |
| 1/2 teaspoon | dried fine herbs *(mix of parsley, chives, tarragon)* | 2 mL |
| pinch | cayenne | pinch |
| 2 cups | milk | 500 mL |
| 2 Tablespoons | tapioca starch | 30 mL |

- Place in stockpot: potatoes, onions, water, salt, pepper. Bring to boil, reduce heat, cover, simmer for 12 minutes. Add scallops, peas, marjoram leaves, fine herbs, cayenne. Stir in milk slowly. Add tapioca starch – to which you have stirred in a small amount of the hot soup. Simmer for 5 minutes.
- Serves 6-8

*100 Gluten Free Soups*

1 Shrimp Bisque
2 Halibut Chowder
3 Montreal Chowder

Fish Chowder / 43

## Shrimp Bisque

| | | |
|---|---|---|
| 4 1/2 cups | boiling water | 1 L |
| 2 Tablespoons | gluten free chicken soup base | 30 mL |
| 2 Tablespoons | olive oil | 30 mL |
| 1 | leek, *white part only, chopped* | 1 |
| 1 | onion, *chopped* | 1 |
| 1 clove | garlic, *chopped* | 1 clove |
| 1 Tablespoon | potato flour | 15 mL |
| 1/3 cup | white wine | 75 mL |
| 2 Tablespoons | potato starch | 30 mL |
| 1/3 cup | cold water | 75 mL |
| 2/3 cup | V8 *or other vegetable juice* | 150 mL |
| 1 Tablespoon | tomato paste | 15 mL |
| 1 teaspoon | sugar | 5 mL |
| 1 1/2 cups | shrimp, *peeled, cooked* | 375 mL |
| 1 teaspoon | dried dill weed | 5 mL |
| 1/8 teaspoon | cayenne | 0.5 mL |
| 1/2 cup | 35% cream | 125 mL |
| 1/2 cup | milk | 125 mL |

- Mix chicken soup base into boiling water, simmer for 1 minute. Set aside.
- Place olive oil in warm fry pan. Add leek, onion, garlic, stir and cook for 3-4 minutes. Add flour, then white wine, continuing to stir and cook for 1 minute. Add to soup base dissolved in water.
- In a separate dish, mix together potato starch and cold water, stir into soup, first adding a little of the hot soup to it.
- To the above, add remaining ingredients, stir, bring to boil, reduce heat, simmer for 5 minutes.
- Serves 5

## Halibut Chowder

| | | |
|---|---|---|
| 1 lb | **halibut,** *bones, skin and flesh* | 500 g |
| 4 cups | water | 1 L |
| | | |
| 4 cups | water | 1 L |
| 3 Tablespoons | gluten free chicken soup base | 45 mL |
| | | |
| 2 | **carrots,** *peeled and chopped* | 2 |
| 2 | **potatoes,** *peeled and chopped* | 2 |
| 2 stalks | **celery,** *strings removed, chopped* | 2 stalks |
| 1 | **leek,** *chopped* | 1 |
| 1/2 | **red pepper,** *peeled and chopped* | 1/2 |
| 1 | **tomato,** *peeled and chopped* | 1 |
| | | |
| 4 Tablespoons | tapioca starch | 60 mL |
| 1/3 cup | cold water | 75 mL |
| | | |
| 1 cup | 15% cream | 250 mL |

- Place halibut bones, skin and flesh in 4 cups (1 L) water. Bring to boil, reduce heat, cover, simmer for 30 minutes. Strain into a bowl, reserve cooking water, discard bones and skin, set aside halibut flesh.

- In a separate stockpot, bring 4 cups (1 L) water to the boil, stir in chicken soup base, simmer for 3 minutes. Add reserved cooking water. Add vegetables, return to boil, reduce heat, cover, simmer for 20 minutes. Blend with hand blender.

- In a small dish, stir tapioca flour into 1/3 cup (75 mL) cold water, and stir into soup, first adding a little of the hot mixture to it. Simmer for 5 minutes.

- Add cream and reserved halibut flesh – which has been carefully picked over for bones. Simmer for 3 minutes.

- Serves 8

## Montreal Chowder

| | | |
|---|---|---|
| 1 lb | halibut & doré, *bones, skin and flesh* | 500 g |
| 4 cups | water | 1 L |
| 2 | bay leaves | 2 |
| 1/2 teaspoon | salt | 2 mL |
| 1 | onion, *chopped* | 1 |
| 2 | carrots, *peeled and sliced* | 2 |
| 2 | potatoes, *peeled and diced* | 2 |
| 2 | tomatoes, *peeled and chopped* | 2 |
| 1 | leek, *chopped* | 1 |
| 1 | orange pepper, *peeled and chopped* | 1 |
| 3 cups | water | 750 mL |
| 4 Tablespoons | tapioca starch | 60 mL |
| 1/2 cup | water | 125 mL |
| 3/4 lb | raw shrimp | 375 g |
| 1/4 lb | raw tilapia *(or other fish fillet), cut into small pieces* | 125 g |
| 3/4 cup | V8 *(or tomato juice)* | 175 mL |
| 1/2 teaspoon | salt | 2 mL |
| 1/2 teaspoon | lemon pepper | 2 mL |
| 3 cups | reserved fish stock | 750 mL |

- Place fish bones, skin, flesh, water, bay leaves, salt, onion in stockpot. Bring to boil, reduce heat, cover and simmer for 25 minutes. Strain - reserving stock. Carefully feel fish, discarding bones, skin and 2 bay leaves. Set flesh aside – in refrigerator.

- Place carrots, potatoes, tomatoes, leek, orange pepper in 3 cups (750 mL) water in large stockpot. Bring to boil, reduce heat, cover, simmer for 15 minutes.

- In a separate dish, stir 1/2 cup (125 mL) water into tapioca starch and add it to vegetables in stockpot, first adding a little of the hot mixture to it.

- Add shrimp, tilapia, V8, salt, lemon pepper, reserved fish stock. Bring to boil, reduce heat, cover, simmer for 8 minutes. Add reserved halibut and doré flesh, continue to simmer for 2 minutes.

- Serves 6

# LENTILS, SPLIT PEAS, BEANS, CHICK PEAS

*LENTIL SOUP*

*VEGETARIAN RED LENTIL SOUP*

*RED LENTIL SOUP*

*GREEN LENTIL SOUP*

*BLENDED LENTIL SOUP*

*(5 pictures, page 48)*

*YELLOW SPLIT PEA SOUP*

*GREEN LENTIL AND GREEN SPLIT PEA SOUP*

*GREEN SPLIT PEA SOUP*

*BLENDED GREEN LENTIL SOUP*

*YELLOW AND GREEN SPLIT PEA SOUP*

*(5 pictures, page 53)*

*FOUR BEAN SOUP*

*ZUCCHINI BEAN SOUP*

*WHITE KIDNEY BEAN SOUP*

*SIX BEAN SOUP*

*(4 pictures, page 58)*

*QUICK AND CHUNKY CHICK PEA SOUP*

*SQUASH SOUP WITH CHICK PEAS*

*MULTI-VEGETABLE SOUP WITH CHICK PEAS*

*CHICK PEA SOUP*

*SPAGHETTI SQUASH SOUP WITH RED LENTILS*

*(5 pictures, page 61)*

1. Lentil Soup
2. Vegetarian Red Lentil Soup
3. Red Lentil Soup
4. Green Lentil Soup
5. Blended Lentil Soup

## Lentil Soup

| | | |
|---|---|---|
| 7 cups | cold water | 1.6 L |
| 1 | veal shank | 1 |
| 1 | onion, *chopped* | 1 |
| 1 teaspoon | salt | 5 mL |
| 3 | bay leaves | 3 |
| 1 Tablespoon | apple cider vinegar | 15 mL |
| 2/3 cup | lentils, *washed* | 150 mL |
| 2 | leeks, *chopped* | 2 |
| 4 | carrots, *peeled and sliced* | 4 |
| 2 cloves | garlic, *peeled and chopped* | 2 cloves |
| 2 cups | tinned ground tomatoes | 500 mL |
| 1/2 teaspoon | salt | 2 mL |
| 1/8 teaspoon | white pepper | 0.5 mL |
| 1 teaspoon | celery salt | 5 mL |
| 2 pinches | cayenne | 2 pinches |
| 1/2 teaspoon | dried basil | 2 mL |
| 1/2 teaspoon | dried thyme | 2 mL |
| 1 Tablespoon | olive oil | 15 mL |
| 2 Tablespoons | sugar | 30 mL |

- To boiling water in large stockpot, add veal shank, onion, salt, bay leaves and apple cider vinegar. Return to boil, reduce heat, cover, simmer for 30 minutes. Add lentils, simmer for another 30 minutes.
- Add all other ingredients, return to boil, reduce heat, cover, simmer for 30 minutes. Remove bone, meat and 3 bay leaves. Discard bone and bay leaves, use meat for sandwiches.
- Serves 6

*If I just say "lentils" in a recipe then it means brown lentils, otherwise I would say red or green lentils.*

## Vegetarian Red Lentil Soup

| | | |
|---|---|---|
| 1/2 cup | red lentils, *washed* | 125 mL |
| 1/2 cup | basmati brown rice, *washed* | 125 mL |
| 9 cups | water | 2 L |
| 2 | carrots, *peeled and chopped* | 2 |
| 1 | onion, *peeled and chopped* | 1 |
| 1 cup | red cabbage, *chopped* | 250 mL |
| 1 clove | garlic, *peeled and chopped* | 1 clove |
| 1 teaspoon | salt | 5 mL |
| 1/2 teaspoon | dried tarragon | 2 mL |
| 1/2 teaspoon | dried thyme | 2 mL |
| 1/2 teaspoon | celery salt | 2 mL |
| 1/4 teaspoon | dried sage | 1 mL |

- Place in stockpot: lentils, rice and water. Bring to boil, reduce heat, cover, simmer for 1 hour. Add all other ingredients. Return to boil, reduce heat, cover, simmer for 30 minutes or until vegetables are tender. Blend with hand blender.
- Serves 6

## Red Lentil Soup

| | | |
|---|---|---|
| 9 cups | cold water | 2 L |
| 3 Tablespoons | gluten free chicken soup base | 45 mL |
| 2 Tablespoons | olive oil | 30 mL |
| 2 | apples, *peeled and chopped* | 2 |
| 1 large | leek, *chopped* | 1 large |
| 2 Tablespoons | gluten free flour mix *(see page vii)* | 30 mL |
| 2 cups | red lentils, *washed* | 500 mL |
| 1/4 teaspoon | dried ginger | 1 mL |
| pinch | cayenne | pinch |

- Add soup base to boiling water, reduce heat, simmer for 3 minutes. Set aside. In separate pan, fry apples and leek for 5 minutes in olive oil, add flour, stir and continue to cook for 2 more minutes.
- Add apple-leek mix to soup base in boiling water, then add red lentils, ginger and cayenne. Bring to boil, reduce heat, cover, simmer for 30 minutes until lentils are cooked. Blend with hand blender. Test for salt and add if required. (Some soup bases have salt and some do not.)
- Serves 7

## Green Lentil Soup

| | | |
|---|---|---|
| 1 cup | green lentils, *rinsed* | 250 mL |
| 1 | leek, *chopped fine* | 1 |
| 2 | apples | 2 |
| 2/3 cup | grapefruit juice | 150 mL |
| 8 cups | vegetable stock *(see page 115)* | 2 L |
| 2 cloves | garlic, *crushed* | 2 cloves |
| 1 1/4 teaspoons | salt | 6 mL |
| 1/4 teaspoon | thyme | 1 mL |
| 1/8 teaspoon | white pepper | 0.5 mL |
| 1/8 teaspoon | cayenne | 0.5 mL |
| 2 Tablespoons | sugar | 30 mL |
| 1 large | zucchini, *peeled and diced* | 1 large |

- As apples are peeled and diced, immerse them immediately in the grapefruit juice.
- Place all ingredients, except zucchini, in large stockpot, bring to boil, reduce heat, cover, simmer for 25 minutes.
- Add zucchini, return to boil, reduce heat, simmer for 5 minutes.
- Serves 8

*Lentils are great – red, green, brown – all are good. And good for you, especially if you want to cut down on meat. Soups made with lentils, beans, split peas, chick peas are all very nourishing and filling and delicious.*

*This is a Vegetarian Soup.*

## Blended Lentil Soup

| | | |
|---|---|---|
| 1 | lamb bone | 1 |
| 9 cups | water | 2 L |
| 2 | onions, *peeled and sliced* | 2 |
| 3/4 cup | lentils, *washed* | 185 mL |
| 5 | carrots, *peeled and sliced* | 5 |
| 4 | bay leaves | 4 |
| 1 1/4 teaspoons | salt | 6 mL |
| 2 Tablespoons | gluten free flour mix *(see page vii)* | 30 mL |
| 2 Tablespoons | olive oil | 30 mL |
| 4 Tablespoons | tomato paste | 60 mL |
| 1/2 teaspoon | dried basil leaves | 2 mL |
| 1/2 teaspoon | dried oregano leaves | 2 mL |
| 1/2 teaspoon | dried thyme leaves | 2 mL |
| pinch | cayenne | pinch |

- Place in large stock pot: lamb bone, water, onions, lentils, carrots, bay leaves and salt. Bring to boil, reduce heat, cover, simmer for 1 hour. Remove and discard 4 bay leaves. Remove lamb bone, take meat off and use separately, discard bone. Blend soup with hand blender.

- In a separate dish, stir flour and olive oil together and stir into soup – first adding a little of the hot mixture to it. Add all seasonings. Return to boil, reduce heat, cover, simmer for 7 minutes. Give a quick blend if necessary.

- Serves 7

*This is a blended lentil soup – which is really nice and so smooth. To replace the 9 cups (2 L) water you could put 9 cups (2L) lamb stock (see page 112). It will give the soup more of a lamb flavour. Try it each way and see which you prefer.*

*100 Gluten Free Soups*

1. Yellow Split Pea Soup
2. Green Lentil & Green Split Pea Soup
3. Green Split Pea Soup
4. Blended Green Lentil Soup
5. Yellow & Green Split Pea Soup

Lentils, Split Peas, Beans, Chick Peas / 53

## Yellow Split Pea Soup

| 8 cups | cold water | 2 L |
| 1 | veal shank | 1 |
| 2 | bay leaves | 2 |
| 1/2 teaspoon | salt | 2 mL |
| 1 | onion, *peeled and chopped* | 1 |
| 1 cup | carrots, *peeled and sliced thin* | 250 mL |
| 1 cup | celery, *strings removed, chopped* | 250 mL |
| 1 cup | yellow split peas, *rinsed* | 250 mL |
| 1 teaspoon | dried thyme | 5 mL |
| pinch | cayenne | pinch |
| pinch | white pepper | pinch |

- To boiling water add veal shank, bay leaves, salt and onion. Reduce heat, cover, simmer for 30 minutes.
- Add remaining ingredients, return to boil, reduce heat, cover, simmer for 45 minutes.
- Remove bone, meat and 2 bay leaves. Discard bone and bay leaves. Use the meat for sandwiches. Blend soup with hand blender.
- Serves 6

*The veal shank and the yellow split peas give a different taste. The hand blender is so handy. The thyme gives a distinctive flavour.*

## GREEN LENTIL & GREEN SPLIT PEA SOUP

| | | |
|---|---|---|
| 1/2 cup | green lentils, *washed* | 125 mL |
| 1/2 cup | green split peas, *washed* | 125 mL |
| 8 cups | water | 2 L |
| 2 | onions, *chopped* | 2 |
| 2 | chicken thighs, *skin and fat removed* | 2 |
| 1 1/4 teaspoons | salt | 6 mL |
| 1 cup | tinned ground tomatoes | 250 mL |
| 3 stalks | celery, *strings removed, chopped* | 3 stalks |
| 1/2 bunch | fresh parsley, *tied in cheesecloth* | 1/2 bunch |
| 1 teaspoon | dried ginger | 5 mL |
| 1/2 teaspoon | celery salt | 2 mL |
| 1/8 teaspoon | white pepper | 0.5 mL |
| 2 pinches | cayenne | 2 pinches |
| 1 teaspoon | dried dill weed | 5 mL |
| 1 Tablespoon | sugar | 15 mL |
| 1/4 teaspoon | dried coriander | 1 mL |

- In stockpot place lentils, split peas, water, onions, chicken thighs and salt. Bring to boil, reduce heat, cover, simmer for 40 minutes.
- Add remaining ingredients, return to boil, reduce heat, cover, simmer for another 40 minutes. Remove and discard parsley tied in cheesecloth.
- Remove chicken and bones, discard bones, chop chicken in small pieces and return to soup. Blend soup with hand blender.
- Serves 6

*The chicken thighs, green lentils and green split peas make a good combination. The vegetables and mixed seasonings round out the soup. The mix makes a full bodied dish.*

## Green Split Pea Soup

| 8 cups | cold water | 2 L |
|---|---|---|
| 4 Tablespoons | gluten free chicken soup base | 60 mL |
| 3 | carrots, *peeled and sliced* | 3 |
| 3 stalks | celery, *strings removed, chopped* | 3 stalks |
| 1 cup | green split peas | 250 mL |
| 1 Tablespoon | tomato paste | 15 mL |
| 1 1/2 teaspoons | dried thyme | 7 mL |
| 1/8 teaspoon | cayenne | 0.5 mL |
| 1/8 teaspoon | white pepper | 0.5 mL |
| 1 teaspoon | sugar | 5 mL |
| 3 Tablespoons | tapioca starch | 45 mL |
| 1/3 cup | water | 75 mL |

- Dissolve soup base in boiling water, stir, reduce heat, simmer for 1 minute. Add remainder of ingredients – except tapioca starch and 1/3 cup (75 mL) water – bring to boil, reduce heat, cover, simmer for 40 minutes. Blend with hand blender.

- In a separate dish, stir water into tapioca starch, add to soup, first adding a little of the hot mixture to it. Give a quick blend with hand blender. Simmer for 7 minutes to cook starch. Taste for salt.

- Serves 6

## Blended Green Lentil Soup

| 6 cups | water | 1.5 L |
|---|---|---|
| 6 teaspoons | gluten free chicken soup base | 30 mL |
| 1/2 cup | green lentils, *washed* | 125 mL |
| 1 | onion, *peeled and chopped* | 1 |
| 1 | leek, *washed and chopped* | 1 |
| 2 | carrots, *peeled and sliced* | 2 |
| 4 stalks | celery, *strings removed, chopped* | 4 stalks |
| 1/2 teaspoon | dried ginger | 2 mL |
| 1/2 teaspoon | dried dill weed | 2 mL |
| 1/4 teaspoon | garlic powder | 1 mL |

- Bring water to boil, add chicken soup base, simmer for 3 minutes. Add lentils, onion, leek, carrots, celery. Return to boil, reduce heat, cover, simmer for 1 hour. Add seasonings, simmer for 5 minutes. Remove from heat. Blend with hand blender.

- Serves 4

## YELLOW AND GREEN SPLIT PEA SOUP

| | | |
|---|---|---|
| 8 cups | cold water | 2 L |
| 8 teaspoons | gluten free chicken soup base | 40 mL |
| 2 | carrots, *peeled and sliced* | 2 |
| 2 large | onions, *peeled and chopped* | 2 large |
| 2/3 cup | yellow split peas, *washed* | 150 mL |
| 1/2 cup | green split peas, *washed* | 125 mL |
| 1 teaspoon | dried Italian seasoning | 5 mL |
| 1 teaspoon | celery salt | 5 mL |
| pinch | white pepper | pinch |
| pinch | cayenne | pinch |
| 3 Tablespoons | brown rice flour mix | 45 mL |
| 2 Tablespoons | olive oil | 30 mL |

*(When using dried chicken soup base – do not add salt until the end – then taste for salt – as each brand differs in amount of salt.)*

- To boiling water add chicken soup base, stir and simmer for 2 minutes.
- Add all ingredients except flour and olive oil. Return to boil, reduce heat, cover and simmer for 1 hour.
- In a separate dish mix flour and olive oil, add a little of the hot mixture to this, then stir this into the soup for thickening. Continue to simmer for 7 minutes – for flour to cook. Taste for salt.
- **Serves 6**  *(Picture on front cover)*

*All these soups – peas, beans, lentils – are so good – and there is such variety here. Try a few and see which you prefer.*

THE GRACIOUS TABLE: SOUPS BY CAROL

1. Four Bean Soup
2. Zucchini Bean Soup
3. White Kidney Bean Soup
4. Six Bean Soup

58 / Lentils, Split Peas, Beans, Chick Peas

## Zucchini Bean Soup

| | | |
|---|---|---|
| 5 1/2 cups | gluten free chicken stock | 1.3 L |
| 2 1/2 cups | water | 625 mL |
| 1 cup | tinned white kidney beans, *drained and rinsed* | 250 mL |
| 2 | onions, *peeled and chopped* | 2 |
| 2 | apples, *peeled and chopped* | 2 |
| 2 medium | zucchini, *peeled and chopped* | 2 medium |
| 1/2 | green pepper, *chopped* | 1/2 |
| 3 Tablespoons | tomato paste | 45 mL |
| 1/8 teaspoon | white pepper | 0.5 mL |
| 1/2 teaspoon | dried ginger | 2 mL |
| 1/4 teaspoon | garlic powder | 1 mL |
| 3/4 teaspoon | salt | 3 mL |
| pinch | cayenne | pinch |
| 2 Tablespoons | maple syrup | 30 mL |

- Place all ingredients in stockpot, bring to boil, reduce heat, cover, simmer for 25 minutes. Blend with hand blender.

- Serves 8

## Four Bean Soup

This soup is made with a tin of 4 beans, cooked and ready for salad or soup. The four beans are: chick peas, red kidney beans, romano beans, black-eyed peas. If you make your own mix be sure they are cooked before putting into soup.

| | | |
|---|---|---|
| 4 1/2 cups | water | 1 L |
| 2 Tablespoons | gluten free chicken soup base | 30 mL |
| 28 oz | tinned tomatoes, *blended* | 796 mL |
| 19 oz | tinned 4 beans, *drained and rinsed* | 540 mL |
| 1 teaspoon | dried tarragon | 5 mL |
| 1 teaspoon | celery salt | 5 mL |
| 1/8 teaspoon | cayenne | 0.5 mL |
| 3 Tablespoons | sugar | 45 mL |
| 2 Tablespoons | maple syrup | 30 mL |

- To boiling water add chicken soup base, simmer for 2 minutes. Add all other ingredients, return to boil, reduce heat, cover, simmer for 20 minutes. Blend with hand blender. Test for salt and add if required. (Some soup bases have salt.)

- Serves 6

## White Kidney Bean Soup

| | | |
|---|---|---|
| 1 | onion, *peeled and chopped* | 1 |
| 2 cloves | garlic, *peeled and chopped* | 2 cloves |
| 1 | leek, *chopped* | 1 |
| 1 | apple, *peeled and chopped* | 1 |
| 1 | yellow pepper, *peeled and chopped* | 1 |
| 1 | tomato, *peeled and chopped* | 1 |
| 2 Tablespoons | olive oil | 30 mL |
| 4 1/2 cups | water | 1 L |
| 2 cups | tinned ground tomatoes | 500 mL |
| 1 cup | cooked white kidney beans, *rinsed* | 250 mL |
| 1 teaspoon | dried thyme | 5 mL |
| 1 teaspoon | salt | 5 mL |
| 1/8 teaspoon | white pepper | 0.5 mL |
| 2 Tablespoons | sugar | 30 mL |
| 1 Tablespoon | balsamic vinegar | 15 mL |

- Fry onion, garlic, leek, apple, yellow pepper, tomato in olive oil for 5 minutes. Add balance of ingredients – except balsamic vinegar – bring to boil, reduce heat, cover, simmer for 12 minutes. Add balsamic vinegar, and continue to simmer for 2 minutes. Blend if desired.
- Serves 6

## Six Bean Soup

This soup is made with a tin of 6 beans, cooked and ready for salad or soup. The six beans are: chick peas, red kidney beans, black-eyed peas, romano beans, baby lima beans, white kidney beans. If you make your own mix be sure beans and peas are cooked before putting into soup.

| | | |
|---|---|---|
| 4 1/2 cups | beef, chicken or pork stock | 1 L |
| 28 oz | tinned tomatoes, *blended* | 796 mL |
| 19 oz | tinned 6 beans, *drained and rinsed* | 540 mL |
| 1/2 teaspoon | dried basil | 2 mL |
| 1/2 teaspoon | dried oregano | 2 mL |
| 2 Tablespoons | sugar | 30 mL |
| pinch | white pepper | pinch |
| pinch | cayenne | pinch |
| 1 Tablespoon | maple syrup | 15 mL |

- Place all ingredients in stockpot, bring to boil, reduce heat, cover, simmer for 20 minutes. Blend with hand blender. Taste for salt – depends on salt in stock used.
- Serves 6

*100 Gluten Free Soups*

1. Quick and Chunky Chick Pea Soup
2. Squash Soup with Chick Peas
3. Multi-Vegetable Soup with Chick Peas
4. Chick Pea Soup
5. Spaghetti Squash Soup with Red Lentils

## Quick and Chunky Chick Pea Soup

| | | |
|---|---|---|
| 7 cups | water | 1.6 L |
| 2 Tablespoons | gluten free chicken soup base | 30 mL |
| 28 oz. | tinned tomatoes, *cut in chunks* | 796 mL |
| 2 Tablespoons | tinned tomato paste | 30 mL |
| 1 cup | tinned chick peas, *drained and rinsed* | 250 mL |
| 2 | carrots, *peeled and sliced thin* | 2 |
| 2 | onions, *peeled and chopped* | 2 |
| 1 | green pepper, *peeled and chopped* | 1 |
| 2 Tablespoons | sugar | 30 mL |
| 1/8 teaspoon | white pepper | 0.5 mL |
| 1/8 teaspoon | cayenne | 0.5 mL |
| 1/2 teaspoon | dried dill weed | 2 mL |
| 1/2 teaspoon | dried basil | 2 mL |

- Bring water to boil in large stockpot, add chicken soup base, stir. Add all other ingredients, bring to boil, reduce heat, cover, simmer for 35 minutes. Taste for salt (different soup bases have different amounts of salt in them) and add if necessary.

- Serves 8

## Squash Soup with Chick Peas

| | | |
|---|---|---|
| 2 Tablespoons | gluten free chicken soup base | 30 mL |
| 7 cups | water | 1.6 L |
| 1 medium | butternut squash, *peeled and cut in pieces* | 1 med |
| 19 oz tin | cooked chick peas | 540 mL |
| 1/2 | red pepper, *chopped* | 1/2 |
| 1 1/2 teaspoons | dried tarragon | 7 mL |
| 1/2 teaspoon | ginger | 2 mL |
| pinch | black pepper | pinch |
| pinch | cayenne pepper | pinch |
| 2 Tablespoons | 35% cream *(optional)* | 30 mL |

- Add soup base to boiling water in stockpot. Simmer for 3 minutes. Add cut up squash. Return to boil, reduce heat, cover, simmer for 15 minutes. Add chick peas and red pepper and simmer for 10 minutes. Blend with hand blender. Add seasonings and stir. Stir in cream. Taste for salt. *(Some soup bases have more salt than others.)*

- Serves 8

## MULTI-VEGETABLE SOUP WITH CHICK PEAS

| | | |
|---|---|---|
| 9 cups | water | 2 L |
| 3 Tablespoons | gluten free chicken soup base | 45 mL |
| 19 oz tin | chick peas, *drained and rinsed* | 540 mL |
| 7-8 cups | frozen mixed vegetables | 1 Kg |
| 1/8 teaspoon | white pepper | 0.5 mL |
| 1/8 teaspoon | cayenne | 0.5 mL |
| 1/8 teaspoon | garlic powder | 0.5 mL |
| 2 teaspoons | dried ginger | 10 mL |
| 2 Tablespoons | arrowroot flour | 30 mL |

- Add chicken soup base to boiling water, simmer for 2 minutes. Add all ingredients (except arrowroot flour) to soup base, bring to boil, reduce heat, cover, simmer for 30 minutes. Blend with hand blender.

- To arrowroot flour in a separate bowl, add 1 cup blended soup and stir. Add this to soup and give it a quick blend. Then return to boil, reduce heat, cover and simmer for 10 minutes (to cook the flour).

- **Taste for salt and add if necessary** *(each chicken soup base varies in quantity of salt needed – very often it doesn't need any salt as there is usually salt in it)*.

- Serves 8

*This is a real quick soup – the frozen vegetables make it fast. And the chicken soup base also speeds up the process. And the seasonings bring flavour to it all.*

## Chick Pea Soup

| | | |
|---|---|---|
| 1 | chicken thigh, *skin and fat removed* | 1 |
| 1 large | onion, *peeled and chopped* | 1 large |
| 6 cups | water | 1.5 L |
| 1/2 teaspoon | salt | 2 mL |
| 1 clove | garlic, *peeled and chopped* | 1 clove |
| 2 stalks | celery, *strings removed, chopped* | 2 stalks |
| 1 | red pepper, *skinned and chopped* | 1 |
| 2 | carrots, *peeled and thinly sliced* | 2 |
| 1 cup | tinned ground tomatoes | 250 mL |
| 1 cup | tinned chick peas, *drained and rinsed* | 250 mL |
| 1/2 teaspoon | dried basil | 2 mL |
| 1/2 teaspoon | dried dill weed | 2 mL |
| 2 Tablespoons | sugar | 30 mL |
| 2 pinches | white pepper | 2 pinches |
| 2 pinches | cayenne | 2 pinches |

- Place in stockpot: chicken thigh, onion, water, salt. Bring to boil, reduce heat, cover, simmer for 45 minutes.
- Add the remainder of ingredients. Bring to boil, reduce heat, cover, simmer for 30 minutes. Remove chicken thigh, discard bones, chop chicken into small pieces and return it to soup.
- Serves 6

*We don't blend this one – just to give us some variety in the consistency. There are lots of vegetables and seasonings.*

## Spaghetti Squash Soup with Red Lentils

| | | |
|---|---|---|
| 1 large | spaghetti squash | 1 large |
| 1 cup | red lentils, *washed* | 250 mL |
| 7 cups | water | 1.6 mL |
| 1 teaspoon | salt | 5 mL |
| 6 cloves | garlic, *peeled and chopped* | 6 cloves |
| 1 teaspoon | dried ginger | 5 mL |
| 1/4 cup | maple syrup | 60 mL |
| 1/2 cup | 35% cream | 125 mL |

- Place unpeeled spaghetti squash in large pot with enough water to cover it. Bring to boil, reduce heat, cover, simmer for 1 1/4 hours. Remove from water, cut in half lengthwise, scoop out and discard seeds. Scoop out squash and set aside. *(Should yield approximately 6 cups (1.4 L) cooked squash.)*
- Place red lentils, water and salt in large stockpot. Bring to boil, reduce heat, cover, simmer for 30 minutes.
- Add cooked squash, garlic, ginger, maple syrup. Return to boil, reduce heat, cover, simmer for 15 minutes. Blend with hand blender. Stir in cream and serve.
- Serves 10

*This is quite a nice soup – with spaghetti squash and red lentils. Where I say to cook the spaghetti squash for an hour and a quarter you can instead cook it in your microwave (by its directions) and then jump into my soup directions.*

# VEGETABLE SOUPS without Meat

CUCUMBER CARROT SOUP
BROCCOLI PARSLEY SOUP
GREEN SOUP
GINGER CARROT SOUP

*(4 pictures, page 68)*

ORANGE CARROT SOUP

*(picture on front cover)*

ORANGE TURNIP SOUP

*(picture on back cover)*

ONION SOUP
FRENCH ONION SOUP

*(2 pictures, page 74)*

PARSNIP SOUP WITH MINT
TOMATO RICE SOUP
GINGER VEGETABLE SOUP THICK AND HOT

*(3 pictures, page 76)*

HEARTY VEGETABLE SOUP
STRAWBERRY VEGETABLE SOUP
PEPPERPOT SOUP
TOMATO VEGETABLE SOUP

*(4 pictures, page 79)*

1. Cucumber Carrot Soup
2. Broccoli Parsley Soup
3. Green Soup
4. Ginger Carrot Soup

## Cucumber Carrot Soup

| | | |
|---|---|---|
| 8 cups | water | 1.8 L |
| 1 teaspoon | salt | 5 mL |
| 8 | carrots, *peeled and sliced* | 8 |
| 1 | English cucumber, *peeled and chopped* | 1 |
| 1 | onion, *peeled and chopped* | 1 |
| 2 cups | milk | 500 mL |
| 1/8 teaspoon | white pepper | 0.5 mL |
| 2 teaspoons | dried dill weed | 10 mL |
| 1 teaspoon | celery salt | 5 mL |
| 1/4 teaspoon | dried ginger | 1 mL |
| 3 Tablespoons | sugar | 45 mL |
| 1/8 teaspoon | cayenne | 0.5 mL |
| 1/3 cup | arrowroot flour | 75 mL |
| 1/3 cup | cold water | 75 mL |
| 1 cup | orange juice | 250 mL |
| 1/4 cup | maple syrup | 60 mL |

- To boiling water add salt, carrots, cucumber and onion. Return to boil, reduce heat, cover, simmer until carrots are tender – about 25 minutes. Blend with hand blender.
- Add milk gradually and seasonings, stir.
- To thicken, in a separate dish, stir 1/3 cup (75 mL) cold water into flour. Add to soup, first adding a little of the hot mixture to it.
- Add orange juice gradually to soup, stirring constantly, add maple syrup. Bring to boil, reduce heat, simmer for 5 minutes.
- Serves 10

## Broccoli Parsley Soup

| | | |
|---|---|---|
| 9 cups | cold water | 2 L |
| 1/3 cup | brown rice | 75 mL |
| 1 1/2 heads | broccoli, *flowerets with short stem* | 1 1/2 heads |
| 2 Tablespoons | olive oil | 30 mL |
| 2 cups | milk | 500 mL |
| pinch | cayenne | pinch |
| 1 teaspoon | celery salt | 5 mL |
| 1/4 teaspoon | dried ginger | 1 mL |
| 1/2 teaspoon | onion powder | 2 mL |
| 1/2 teaspoon | salt | 2 mL |
| pinch | white pepper | pinch |
| 1/3 cup | fresh parsley, *finely chopped* | 75 mL |
| 1 | zucchini for topping | 1 |

- To boiling water in large stockpot add rice and broccoli. Return to boil, reduce heat, cover, simmer for 20 minutes. Blend with hand blender.
- Add remainder of ingredients – except zucchini – return to boil, reduce heat, cover, simmer for 7 minutes. Serve topped with grated raw zucchini.
- Serves 8

*This is such a popular soup – Broccoli – that I have 3 versions of it – chicken, ginger, parsley. Try them and see which you prefer. One has chicken, one chicken soup base, and one is without meat.*

## Green Soup

| | | |
|---|---|---|
| 9 cups | water | 2 L |
| 1 | Romaine lettuce | 1 |
| 2 pkgs (300g each) | frozen spinach | 600 g |
| 1 bunch | celery hearts, *chopped* | 1 bunch |
| 1/2 | English cucumber, *peeled and chopped* | 1/2 |
| 1/2 head | broccoli, *flowerets with short stem* | 1/2 head |
| 1 large | onion, *chopped* | 1 large |
| 1 teaspoon | celery salt | 5 mL |
| 1 teaspoon | dried dill weed | 5 mL |
| 1 teaspoon | salt | 5 mL |
| 1 Tablespoon | sugar | 15 mL |
| 1/8 teaspoon | white pepper | 0.5 mL |
| 1/8 teaspoon | garlic powder | 0.5 mL |
| 2 pinches | cayenne | 2 pinches |
| 2 Tablespoons | sour cream | 30 mL |

- Place water and all vegetables in large stockpot. Bring to boil, reduce heat, add seasonings, cover, simmer for 30 minutes. Blend with hand blender. Add sour cream and blend again quickly.
- Serves 10

## Ginger Carrot Soup

| | | |
|---|---|---|
| 11 | carrots, *peeled and sliced* | 11 |
| 5 cups | water | 1.2 L |
| 1/2 teaspoon | salt | 2 mL |
| 2 1/2 cups | milk | 625 mL |
| 1 1/2 teaspoons | dried ginger | 7 mL |
| 1/2 cup | maple syrup | 125 mL |
| 3 Tablespoons | brown rice flour mix | 45 mL |

- To boiling water add chicken soup base, simmer for 2 minutes. Add all other ingredients, return to boil, reduce heat, cover, simmer for 20 minutes. Blend with hand blender. Test for salt and add if required. *(Some soup bases have salt.)*
- Serves 6

## Orange Carrot Soup

| | | |
|---|---|---|
| 8 | carrots, *peeled and sliced* | 8 |
| 1 cup | water | 250 mL |
| 1 1/2 Tablespoons | olive oil | 22 mL |
| 2 Tablespoons | gluten free flour mix *(see page vii)* | 30 mL |
| 1 cup | water | 250 mL |
| 2 cups | water | 500 mL |
| 1 1/2 cups | milk | 375 mL |
| 1 1/2 cups | orange juice | 375 mL |
| 1 1/2 Tablespoons | sugar | 22 mL |
| 3/4 teaspoon | celery salt | 3 mL |
| 7/8 teaspoon | salt | 4 mL |
| 1 teaspoon | dried dill weed | 5 mL |
| 1 teaspoon | dried ginger | 5 mL |
| pinch | cayenne | pinch |
| pinch | white pepper | pinch |

- Cook carrots in pressure cooker for 3 minutes or boil them in water until tender. In either case, reserve cooking water and use in the water called for below. Cool cooked carrots and blend in food processor with 1 cup (250 mL) water. Set aside.

- In a small bowl, over medium heat, mix olive oil and flour, slowly adding 1 cup (250 mL) water. Stir into a paste for thickening the soup. Set aside.

- In stockpot over medium high heat – place 2 cups (500 mL) water, milk, blended carrots, stir. Add orange juice slowly, while stirring constantly. Bring to boil. Stir in thickened paste – first adding a little of the hot mixture to the paste.

- Add seasonings, return to boil, reduce heat, simmer for 5 minutes.

- Note: Total water is 1 cup (250 mL) in blending carrots, plus 1 cup (250 mL) for thickening, plus 2 cups (500 mL) in soup – 4 cups (1 L) in all.

- **Serves 6** *(Picture on front cover)*

## ORANGE TURNIP SOUP

| | | |
|---|---|---|
| 1 med-large | turnip | 1 med-large |
| 1 cup | water | 250 mL |
| 1 Tablespoon | olive oil | 15 mL |
| 2 Tablespoons | gluten free flour mix *(see page vii)* | 30 mL |
| 4 cups | cold water/reserved cooking water | 1 L |
| 2 cups | milk | 500 mL |
| 2 Tablespoons | maple syrup | 30 mL |
| 1/2 teaspoon | celery salt | 2 mL |
| 1/2 teaspoon | dried ginger | 2 mL |
| 1/2 teaspoon | salt | 2 mL |
| 1/4 teaspoon | dried coriander | 1 mL |
| 1 Tablespoon | sugar | 15 mL |
| pinch | cayenne | pinch |
| 1 1/2 cups | orange juice | 375 mL |

- Peel, cut and cook turnip in water until tender or cook in pressure cooker for 8 minutes. Reserve cooking water. Blend turnip in food processor or blender with 1 cup (250 mL) water. Set aside.

- Over medium heat in large stockpot – make a paste of olive oil and flour, gradually add the 4 cups (1 L) water, stirring constantly. Add remainder of ingredients – milk first, maple syrup, blended turnip, seasonings while stirring. Add orange juice slowly at the last, stirring constantly. Bring to boil, reduce heat, cover, simmer for 5-7 minutes.

- Serves 8 *(Picture on back cover)*

*Some people are not fond of turnip soup but with the orange juice and the seasonings in it, Orange Turnip Soup can be quite lovely.*

THE GRACIOUS TABLE: SOUPS BY CAROL

1 ONION SOUP
2 FRENCH ONION SOUP

74 / VEGETABLE SOUPS WITHOUT MEAT

## Onion Soup

| | | |
|---|---|---|
| 10 large | onions, *peeled and sliced in rings* | 10 large |
| 1/4 cup | olive oil | 60 mL |
| 9 cups | vegetable stock *(see page 115)* | 2 L |
| 9 cups | water | 2 L |
| 1 teaspoon | garlic powder | 5 mL |
| 1/2 teaspoon | white pepper | 2 mL |
| 1 teaspoon | salt | 5 mL |
| 1/8 teaspoon | cayenne | 0.5 mL |

- Fry onions in olive oil for 10-12 minutes, until cooked and lightly browned. Place onions and all other ingredients in large stockpot. Bring to boil, reduce heat, cover, simmer for 15 minutes. Taste for salt – you may want to add a little – but if you are serving it as French Onion Soup *(see below)* you will not want to, as the cheese has salt in it.

- Serves 15

## French Onion Soup

| | | |
|---|---|---|
| 15 cups | onion soup *(see above)* | 3.4 L |
| 10 slices | gluten free bread or crisp bread | 10 slices |
| 1 1/2 cups | grated skim milk mozzarella cheese | 375 mL |
| 1/2 cup | very finely grated parmesan cheese | 125 mL |

- Ladle soup into 10 onion soup bowls, top each with slice of gluten free bread, sprinkle grated mozzarella cheese over bread, and top with sprinkling of grated parmesan. Place in preheated 350 degree oven for 15 minutes or until cheese is melted and bubbly and nicely browned.

- Serves 10

*Onion Soup is one of my favorite soups – especially French Onion Soup.*

THE GRACIOUS TABLE: SOUPS BY CAROL

1   Parsnip Soup with Mint
2   Tomato Rice Soup
3   Ginger Vegetable Soup Thick and Hot

## Parsnip Soup with Mint

| 6 cups | water | 1.4 L |
|---|---|---|
| 7 | **parsnips,** *peeled and sliced* | 7 |
| 1 cup | **chopped celery,** *strings removed* | 250 mL |
| 1 | **onion,** *peeled and chopped* | 1 |
| 1 | **green pepper,** *peeled and chopped* | 1 |
| 3 | **apples,** *peeled and chopped* | 3 |
| 1 teaspoon | salt | 5 mL |
| pinch | cayenne | pinch |
| 1 teaspoon | crushed dried mint | 5 mL |
| 1 Tablespoon | maple syrup | 15 mL |

- Place all ingredients in stockpot, bring to boil, reduce heat, cover, simmer for 25 minutes, or until vegetables are tender. Blend with hand blender.
- Serves 6

## Tomato Rice Soup

| 28 oz | tinned ground tomatoes | 796 mL |
|---|---|---|
| 2 1/2 cups | water | 625 mL |
| 2 1/2 cups | milk | 625 mL |
| 3 Tablespoons | basmati rice | 45 mL |
| 1/2 teaspoon | dried basil | 2 mL |
| 1/8 teaspoon | dried coriander | 0.5 mL |
| 1/8 teaspoon | dried oregano | 0.5 mL |
| 1/2 teaspoon | dried dill weed | 2 mL |
| 1/4 teaspoon | dried ginger | 1 mL |
| 1/4 teaspoon | salt | 1 mL |
| pinch | cayenne | pinch |
| pinch | black pepper | pinch |
| 3 Tablespoons | sugar | 45 mL |
| 5 Tablespoons | maple syrup | 75 mL |

- Place all ingredients in stockpot, bring to boil, reduce heat, cover, simmer, for 30 minutes – until rice is cooked.
- Serves 5

## Ginger Vegetable Soup Thick and Hot

| | | |
|---|---|---|
| 3/4 cup | water | 175 mL |
| 1/4 cup | brown rice | 60 mL |
| 1/4 teaspoon | salt | 1 mL |
| 1/2 cup | water | 125 mL |
| 1/2 small | cauliflower | 1/2 small |
| 1/2 small | broccoli, *flowerets with short stem* | 1/2 small |
| 1/2 | English cucumber, *peeled* | 1/2 |
| 1 | onion | 1 |
| 2 stalks | celery, *strings removed* | 2 stalks |
| 3 small | carrots | 3 small |
| 4 slices | fennel | 4 slices |
| 5 cups | cold water | 1.2 L |
| 1 cup | milk | 250 mL |
| 1/2 teaspoon | celery salt | 2 mL |
| 1/2 teaspoon | dried ginger | 2 mL |
| 1 1/2 teaspoons | dried dill weed | 7 mL |
| 1/4 teaspoon | garlic powder | 1 mL |
| 1 teaspoon | salt | 5 mL |
| 2 pinches | white pepper | 2 pinches |
| 2 pinches | cayenne | 2 pinches |
| 1/2 teaspoon | fennel seeds | 2 mL |
| 1 teaspoon | lemon pepper | 5 mL |
| 1/2 cup | orange juice | 125 mL |

- To 3/4 cup (175 mL) boiling water add rice and salt, reduce heat, cover, simmer for 20 minutes. Cool and liquefy in blender with 1/2 cup (125 mL) water.
- Chop all vegetables and cook in 5 cups (1.2 L) boiling water for 20 minutes. Blend with hand blender.
- Add blended rice to blended vegetables in large stockpot, add milk and seasonings, stir in orange juice last. Bring to the boil, reduce heat, simmer for 5 minutes.
- Serves 6

*100 Gluten Free Soups*

1. Hearty Vegetable Soup
2. Strawberry Vegetable Soup
3. Pepperpot Soup
4. Tomato Vegetable Soup

Vegetable Soups without Meat / 79

## Hearty Vegetable Soup

| | | |
|---|---|---|
| 9 cups | water | 2 L |
| 1/2 small | cauliflower | 1/2 small |
| 1/2 small | broccoli, *flowerets with short stem* | 1/2 small |
| 3 | carrots, *peeled and sliced* | 3 |
| 14 oz tin | tomatoes with juice | 398 mL |
| 1 small | green pepper, *peeled and chopped* | 1 small |
| 1/2 cup | small gluten free pasta | 125 mL |
| 3/4 teaspoon | salt | 3 mL |
| 1 Tablespoon | sugar | 15 mL |
| pinch | white pepper | pinch |

- Bring water to boil, add all ingredients, return to boil, reduce heat, cover, simmer for 15-20 minutes until vegetables are tender.
- Serves 8

## Strawberry Vegetable Soup

| | | |
|---|---|---|
| 2 | onions, *peeled and chopped* | 2 |
| 1 | leek, *white part only, chopped* | 1 |
| 1/2 bunch | celery, *strings removed, chopped* | 1/2 bunch |
| 3 | potatoes, *peeled and cut in pieces* | 3 |
| 1 head | leaf lettuce, *torn apart* | 1 head |
| 1 bunch | flat-leaf parsley, *stems removed, chopped* | 1 bunch |
| 10 cups | water | 2.3 L |
| 25 | strawberries | 25 |
| 1 teaspoon | ginger | 5 mL |
| 1/2 teaspoon | celery salt | 2 mL |
| 2 teaspoons | salt | 10 mL |
| 2 pinches | cayenne | 2 pinches |
| pinch | cinnamon | pinch |
| 2 1/3 Tablespoons | sugar | 35 mL |

- Place in large stockpot: onions, leek, celery, potatoes, lettuce, parsley, water. Bring to boil, reduce heat, simmer for 10 minutes. Add strawberries and seasonings, return to boil, reduce heat, simmer for 10 minutes. Blend with hand blender. Serve as is or with a dollop of sour cream floating on top.
- Serves 10-12

## Pepperpot Soup

This soup is made from the vegetables used in the making of Vegetable Stock. The vegetables have been cooked for 1 1/2 hours to make the stock – so the vitamin content is diminished but the resulting soup is delicious and high in fiber.

| | | |
|---|---|---|
| 9 cups | vegetable stock | 2 L |
| 9 cups | cooked blended vegetables, from Vegetable Stock (see page 115) | 2 L |
| 2 cups | water | 500mL |
| 1 1/2 teaspoons | dried dill weed | 7 mL |
| 3/4 teaspoon | dried coriander | 3 mL |
| 1 1/2 teaspoons | dried ginger | 7 mL |
| 2 teaspoons | salt | 10 mL |
| 1/4 teaspoon | white pepper | 1 mL |
| 1/4 teaspoon | cayenne | 1 mL |
| 1 teaspoon | celery salt | 5 mL |
| 2 Tablespoons | sugar (optional) | 30 mL |
| 1 cup | cream or milk | 250 mL |

- Place all ingredients in stockpot, bring to the boil, reduce heat, cover, simmer for 10 minutes. Taste for salt and pepper.
- Serves 14

*Didn't I tell you it would be delicious?*

## Tomato Vegetable Soup

| | | |
|---|---|---|
| 14 oz | tinned tomatoes | 398 mL |
| 1/3 cup | tomato paste | 75 mL |
| 1/2 | English cucumber, *peeled and grated* | 1/2 |
| 1/2 | Romaine lettuce, *torn apart* | 1/2 |
| 3 stalks | celery, *strings removed, grated* | 3 stalks |
| 4 | carrots, *peeled and grated* | 4 |
| 1 | potato, *peeled and grated* | 1 |
| 13 1/2 cups | water | 3 L |
| 1 teaspoon | salt | 5 mL |
| 1 teaspoon | dried dill weed | 5 mL |
| 1/4 teaspoon | oregano | 1 mL |
| 1/8 teaspoon | white pepper | 0.5 mL |
| 1/4 teaspoon | onion powder | 1 mL |
| 1/4 teaspoon | thyme | 1 mL |
| 1/4 teaspoon | garlic powder | 1 mL |
| 1/4 teaspoon | coriander | 1 mL |
| pinch | cayenne | pinch |
| 2 teaspoons | sugar | 10 mL |

- Place all ingredients in large stockpot. Bring to boil, reduce heat, cover, simmer for 15 minutes. Blend with hand blender.
- Serves 12

*Once you get the vegetables prepared the soup is very quick to cook. Just put in the seasonings and blend and its ready.*

# VEGETABLE SOUPS WITH MEAT

*APPLE ZUCCHINI SOUP*
*CABBAGE CARROT SOUP*
*SPICY CARROT AND APPLE SOUP*
*(3 pictures, page 84)*

*CELERY CHICKEN SOUP*
*CELERY TOMATO SOUP*
*GINGER CHERRY CONSOMMÉ*
*CHICKEN SOUP WITH BROCCOLI*
*(4 pictures, page 87)*

*CHICKEN NOODLE SOUP*
*ZUCCHINI CHICKEN SOUP*
*LEEK AND PARSNIP SOUP*
*WARM GAZPACHO WITH TURKEY*
*(4 pictures, page 91)*

*LEMON CHEDDAR SOUP*
*OLD BONES SOUP*
*MINESTRONE*
*ONION SOUP FOR EIGHT*
*(4 pictures, page 94)*

*MULLIGATAWNY*
*(picture on front cover)*

*PARSNIP VEGETABLE SOUP*
*TURKEY SOUP*
*PARSNIP APPLE SOUP*
*SWEET AND SOUR PORK SOUP*
*(4 pictures, page 100)*

*LEMON VEGETABLE SOUP*
*BLENDED VEGETABLE SOUP*
*VEGETABLE BEEF SOUP*
*TART VEGETABLE SOUP*
*(4 pictures, page 104)*

THE GRACIOUS TABLE: SOUPS BY CAROL

1. Apple Zucchini Soup
2. Cabbage Carrot Soup
3. Spicy Carrot and Apple Soup

84 / Vegetable Soups with Meat

## Apple Zucchini Soup

| | | |
|---|---|---|
| 3 | **apples,** *peeled and sliced* | 3 |
| 3 medium | **zucchini,** *peeled and sliced* | 3 |
| 3 | **onions,** *peeled and sliced* | 3 |
| 2 Tablespoons | olive oil | 30 mL |
| 4 Tablespoons | brown rice flour mix | 60 mL |
| 8 cups | pork stock *(see page 112)* | 1.8 L |
| 1/2 teaspoon | dried cinnamon | 2 mL |
| 1 Tablespoon | maple syrup | 15 mL |
| 1 teaspoon | dried ginger | 5 mL |
| pinch | cayenne | pinch |

- Fry – in stockpot - apples, zucchini and onions in olive oil for 5-8 minutes. Add flour, stir and continue to cook for 3 minutes.
- Add pork stock, cinnamon, maple syrup, ginger and cayenne. Bring to boil, reduce heat, cover, simmer for 15 minutes. Blend with hand blender.
- Taste for salt and add if required (it depends on how much salt is in the pork stock.)
- Serves 6

## Cabbage Carrot Soup

| | | |
|---|---|---|
| 8 cups | cold water | 1.8 L |
| 5 Tablespoons | gluten free chicken soup base | 75 mL |
| 1/2 small | **cabbage,** *shredded* | 1/2 small |
| 4 | **carrots,** *peeled and sliced thin* | 4 |
| 1/2 teaspoon | dried dill weed | 2 mL |
| 1/2 teaspoon | celery salt | 2 mL |
| pinch | cayenne | pinch |

- Bring water to boil, add soup base, simmer for 1 minute. Add remainder of ingredients, return to boil, reduce heat, cover, simmer for 20 minutes. Taste for salt.
- Serves 6-8

## Spicy Carrot and Apple Soup

| | | |
|---|---|---|
| 8 | carrots, *peeled and sliced* | 8 |
| 2 | apples, *peeled and chopped* | 2 |
| 9 cups | chicken stock *(see page 114)* | 2 L |
| 1 | red pepper, *peeled and chopped* | 1 |
| 3 | garlic buds, *peeled and chopped* | 3 |
| 1 Tablespoon | dried ginger | 15 mL |
| 1/2 teaspoon | cinnamon | 2 mL |
| 1/4 teaspoon | dried cloves | 1 mL |
| 1/2 teaspoon | salt | 2 mL |
| 1/8 teaspoon | cayenne | 0.5 mL |
| 4 Tablespoons | maple syrup | 60 mL |
| 3 Tablespoons | brown rice flour mix | 45 mL |

- In large stockpot, place carrots, apples, chicken stock, red pepper, garlic. Bring to boil, reduce heat, cover, simmer for 20 minutes. Blend with hand blender.
- Add ginger, cinnamon, cloves, salt, cayenne, maple syrup. Stir and continue to simmer.
- In separate dish, mix flour with 1/2 cup (125 mL) soup. Stir this gradually into stockpot. Cover and continue to simmer for 10 minutes. Give a quick blend with hand blender if necessary.
- Serves 8

*There are so many carrot soups in the book – you will just have to try a few – cabbage, cucumber, curried, ginger, orange, spicy. This one has interesting seasonings along with garlic buds. Try it.*

*100 Gluten Free Soups*

1. Celery Chicken Soup
2. Celery Tomato Soup
3. Ginger Cherry Consommé
4. Chicken Soup with Broccoli

Vegetable Soups with Meat

## Celery Chicken Soup

| | | |
|---|---|---|
| 6 | chicken wings | 6 |
| 8 cups | cold water | 1.8 L |
| 1 | onion, *chopped* | 1 |
| 1/2 teaspoon | salt | 2 mL |
| 2 | bay leaves | 2 |
| 1 teaspoon | apple cider vinegar | 5 mL |
| 1/2 bunch | celery hearts, *strings removed, chopped* | 1/2 bunch |
| 1/4 cup | soft Italian rice *(arborico)* | 60 mL |
| pinch | cayenne | pinch |
| 1/2 teaspoon | celery salt | 2 mL |
| pinch | white pepper | pinch |

- Place chicken wings, water, onion, salt, bay leaves and vinegar in stockpot, bring to boil, reduce heat, cover, simmer for 1 hour. Remove and discard chicken wings and 2 bay leaves. Place soup in bowl and refrigerate for several hours or overnight to allow fat to congeal on top, remove fat.

- Place soup back in pot, add remainder of ingredients. Bring to boil, reduce heat, cover, simmer until the celery and rice are tender – about 25 minutes. Taste for salt.

- Serves 5-6

*This is a good chicken soup for a patient – the kind that a mother gives to a child – or anyone who needs some comfort food would be glad to have. It is very simple – just chicken, rice, celery and salt and pepper.*

## CELERY TOMATO SOUP

| | | |
|---|---|---|
| 8 cups | cold water | 1.8 L |
| 1 1/2 cups | celery, *finely chopped* | 375 mL |
| 1/4 lb | lean minced beef | 125 g |
| 1 small | chopped onion | 1 small |
| 1/4 cup | carrots, *peeled and sliced* | 60 mL |
| 2 | bay leaves | 2 |
| 5 Tablespoons | tomato paste | 75 mL |
| 1 Tablespoon | sugar | 15 mL |
| 1/2 teaspoon | salt | 2 mL |
| pinch | white pepper | pinch |
| 1 large | tomato, *peeled and chopped* | 1 large |
| 1/3 cup | gluten free small soup noodles | 75 mL |
| 1/2 cup | frozen peas | 125 mL |

- Bring water to boil, add celery, minced beef, onion, carrots, bay leaves, tomato paste, sugar, salt, pepper. Return to boil, reduce heat, cover, simmer for 35 minutes.
- Add tomato, noodles, peas. Return to boil, reduce heat, simmer for 10 minutes. Taste for sugar and salt. (The acidity of tomatoes varies and often more sugar or salt may be required.) Remove 2 bay leaves.
- Serves 7

## GINGER CHERRY CONSOMMÉ

| | | |
|---|---|---|
| 3 3/4 cups | pork stock *(see page 112)* | 925 mL |
| 1 1/2 cups | sour cherry juice | 375 mL |
| 1/4 teaspoon | salt | 1 mL |
| 3/4 teaspoon | dried ginger | 3 mL |
| 2 Tablespoons | maple syrup | 30 mL |
| pinch | cayenne | pinch |
| 3 Tablespoons | arrowroot flour | 45 mL |
| 1/2 cup | water | 125 mL |

- Place in stockpot: pork stock, sour cherry juice, salt, ginger, maple syrup, cayenne. Bring to boil, reduce heat, cover, simmer for 5 minutes.
- In a separate dish, mix flour and water, add a little of the hot soup to this, then add this to soup and stir. Continue to simmer for another 5 minutes.
- Serves 4

## Chicken Soup with Broccoli

### FIRST STEP – CHICKEN STOCK

*N.B. Be sure that any sauce used in cooking the chicken is gluten free.*

| Skin & bones only of | 1 chicken | skin & bones only |
|---|---|---|
| 2 | onions, *peeled and chopped* | 2 |
| 4 | bay leaves | 4 |
| 1/2 teaspoon | salt | 2 mL |
| 8 cups | water | 1.8 L |

- Place all of the above in a stockpot, bring to the boil, reduce heat, cover and simmer for 2 hours. Strain, reserve stock (liquid) – it will yield 6 cups (1.4 L). Discard bones, skin and vegetables; discard 4 bay leaves.

### SECOND STEP – SOUP

| 1 head | broccoli, *flowerets with short stem* | 1 head |
|---|---|---|
| 1/4 cup | arrowroot flour | 60 mL |
| 1/4 cup | water | 60 mL |

- Add broccoli flowerets to reserved chicken stock in stockpot. Bring to the boil, reduce heat, cover, simmer for 15 minutes. Blend with hand blender.
- Mix arrowroot flour with water in small dish – add to soup, first adding a little of the hot mixture to it. Stir, return to boil, reduce heat, simmer for 8 minutes. If any small lumps of thickening remain – give a quick blend with hand blender.
- Serves 4

*100 Gluten Free Soups*

1 CHICKEN NOODLE SOUP
2 ZUCCHINI CHICKEN SOUP
3 LEEK AND PARSNIP SOUP
4 WARM GAZPACHO WITH TURKEY

## Chicken Noodle Soup

| | | |
|---|---|---|
| 3 | chicken thighs, *skin & fat removed* | 3 |
| 10 cups | water | 2.3 L |
| 1 small | chopped onion | 1 small |
| 3 | bay leaves | 3 |
| 1/4 teaspoon | salt | 1 mL |
| small bunch | parsley, *tied together* | small bunch |
| 1 | carrot, *peeled and grated* | 1 |
| 1/2 cup | finely chopped celery | 125 mL |
| 1/4 cup | gluten free soup noodles | 60 mL |
| 1/3 | green pepper, *peeled and chopped* | 1/3 |
| pinch | salt | pinch |
| pinch | white pepper | pinch |

- Cook chicken thighs in boiling water with onion, bay leaves, salt and parsley for 1 hour. Remove meat from bones, chop in small pieces and return chicken to soup, discard bones.
- Add: grated carrot, celery, noodles, green pepper, salt and pepper. Return to boil, reduce heat, cover, simmer for 20 minutes.
- Remove from heat, discard 3 bay leaves and tied parsley.
- Serves 6

## Zucchini Chicken Soup

| | | |
|---|---|---|
| 2 1/2 cups | chicken stock *(see page 114)* | 625 mL |
| 3 cups | water | 750 mL |
| 2 1/2 cups | zucchini, *peeled and grated* | 625 mL |
| 1 medium | onion, *peeled and chopped fine* | 1 medium |
| 1 teaspoon | salt | 5 mL |
| 1/4 teaspoon | garlic powder | 1 mL |
| 1/2 cup | chicken breast, *cooked and diced* | 125 mL |

- Place in stockpot all ingredients except cooked chicken. Bring to boil, reduce heat, cover, simmer for 10 minutes. Add chicken, continue to simmer for 5 minutes.
- Serves 6

## LEEK AND PARSNIP SOUP

| | | |
|---|---|---|
| 7 1/2 cups | water | 1.7 L |
| 2 Tablespoons | gluten free chicken soup base | 30 mL |
| 2 | carrots | 2 |
| 2 | leeks | 2 |
| 2 | potatoes | 2 |
| 2 | apples | 2 |
| 5 | parsnips | 5 |
| 1 | zucchini | 1 |
| 1 teaspoon | dried marjoram | 5 mL |
| pinch | cayenne | pinch |
| 1/2 teaspoon | dried basil | 2 mL |
| 2 Tablespoons | maple syrup | 30 mL |

- Add chicken soup base to boiling water and stir. Add all vegetables, peeled and chopped. Bring to boil, reduce heat, simmer covered for 20 minutes or until vegetables are tender. Blend with hand blender. Add seasonings. Simmer for 5 minutes.
- Serves 6

## WARM GAZPACHO WITH TURKEY

| | | |
|---|---|---|
| 1/2 lb | minced turkey | 227 g |
| 7 cups | water | 1.6 L |
| 1/2 cup | red lentils, *washed* | 125 mL |
| 1 1/4 teaspoons | salt | 6 mL |
| 28 oz | tinned ground tomatoes | 796 mL |
| 3 | leeks, *washed and chopped* | 3 |
| 3/4 cup | frozen small peas | 175 mL |
| 1 cup | apple juice | 250 mL |
| 2 Tablespoons | sugar | 30 mL |
| 2 Tablespoons | maple syrup | 30 mL |
| 1/4 teaspoon | dried coriander | 1 mL |
| 1/2 teaspoon | dried oregano | 2 mL |
| 1/2 teaspoon | dried basil | 2 mL |
| 3/4 teaspoon | dried mint | 3 mL |

- Place all ingredients in stockpot, bring to boil, reduce heat, cover, simmer for 35 minutes. Blend with hand blender – but not a fine blend.
- Serves 8

THE GRACIOUS TABLE: SOUPS BY CAROL

1 Lemon Cheddar Soup
2 Old Bones Soup
3 Minestrone
4 Onion Soup for 8

94 / Vegetable Soups with Meat

## LEMON CHEDDAR SOUP

| | | |
|---|---|---|
| 4 1/2 cups | gluten free chicken stock | 1 L |
| 1 1/2 cups | water | 375 mL |
| 1/3 cup | uncooked basmati rice | 75 mL |
| 2 | eggs | 2 |
| juice of 1 | lemon | juice of 1 |
| 3/4 cup | grated cheddar cheese | 175 mL |
| 1/2 teaspoon | dried basil | 2 mL |
| 1/4 teaspoon | dried ginger | 1 mL |
| 1/4 teaspoon | salt | 1 mL |
| 1/8 teaspoon | white pepper | 0.5 mL |
| 1 Tablespoon | maple syrup | 15 mL |

- Place chicken stock and water in stockpot, bring to boil, add rice, reduce heat, cover and simmer for 20 minutes.
- In a separate dish, beat eggs with lemon juice. Add this to soup, first adding a little of the hot mixture to it.
- Add all other ingredients. Return to boil, reduce heat, cover, simmer for 10 minutes.
- Serves 4

*Lemon Cheddar Soup is not something you see every day. The eggs, lemon and cheese give a different consistency. It is really quite pleasant.*

## Old Bones Soup

| | | |
|---|---|---|
| 1 | ham bone | 1 |
| 1 | pork bone | 1 |
| 1 | lamb bone | 1 |
| 6 quarts | water | 5.3 L |
| 1 Tablespoon | apple cider vinegar | 15 mL |
| 1 | onion, *peeled and sliced* | 1 |
| 6 | carrots, *peeled and sliced* | 6 |
| 3 1/2 cups | celery, *strings removed, chopped* | 875 mL |
| 1/2 head | cauliflower, *in small pieces* | 1/2 head |
| 1/2 head | broccoli, *flowerets with short stem* | 1/2 head |
| 2 | tomatoes, *peeled and chopped* | 2 |
| 1/2 cup | frozen small peas | 125 mL |
| 2 teaspoons | salt | 10 mL |
| 1 1/2 teaspoons | celery salt | 7 mL |
| 1/4 teaspoon | white pepper | 1 mL |
| 1/4 teaspoon | dried thyme | 1 mL |
| 1/2 teaspoon | dried dill weed | 2 mL |

- Bring water to boil in large stockpot, add the 3 bones, apple cider vinegar and onion. Reduce heat, cover, simmer for 1 1/2 hours. Skim fat off top. Remove bones, pick meat off and return meat to soup, discard bones.
- Add the vegetables first that take the longest to cook – carrots first, after 10 minutes add the celery. After another 10 minutes add the cauliflower, broccoli, tomatoes, frozen peas and seasonings, continue to simmer for another 10 minutes.
- Serves 18-20

*My late sister, Mary, who had 8 children, inspired me to concoct this recipe. With 8 children she had bones from many roasts left over, so she froze them and made many pots of delicious soup.*

## MINESTRONE

| | | |
|---|---|---|
| 1 | veal shank | 1 |
| 1 | onion, *peeled and chopped* | 1 |
| 3/4 teaspoon | salt | 3 mL |
| 3 | bay leaves | 3 |
| 12 cups | cold water | 2.7 L |
| 2 1/2 cups | shredded cabbage | 625 mL |
| 3/4 cup | celery, *strings removed, chopped* | 175 mL |
| 2 cups | carrots, *peeled and sliced thin* | 500 mL |
| 1 cup | cauliflower, *cut in small pieces* | 250 mL |
| 14 oz | tinned tomatoes, *blended* | 420 mL |
| 3 Tablespoons | tomato paste | 45 mL |
| 1 1/4 Tablespoons | sugar | 19 mL |
| 1/4 teaspoon | dried basil | 1 mL |
| 1/4 teaspoon | dried oregano | 1 mL |
| 1/8 teaspoon | dried coriander | 0.5 mL |
| 3/4 teaspoon | dried dill weed | 3 mL |

- Place in stockpot: veal shank, onion, salt, bay leaves and water. Bring to boil, reduce heat, cover, simmer for 1 hour and 20 minutes. Prepare vegetables while soup is cooking.

- Remove meat, bones and 3 bay leaves. Cut meat in bite size pieces and return to soup. Discard bones and bay leaves.

- Add remaining ingredients to soup, return to boil, reduce heat, cover, simmer for 20-30 minutes or until vegetables are just tender.

- Serves 10

*Minestrone is a favorite for many people. There are many varieties of it – try mine.*

## Onion Soup for Eight

This recipe is a quick way to make onion soup – and every bit as delicious. The difference is in the gluten free chicken soup base rather than the Vegetable Stock and it has a little sweetener in it.

| | | |
|---|---|---|
| 8 cups | water | 1.8 L |
| 2 1/2 Tablespoons | gluten free chicken soup base | 37 mL |
| 5 | onions, *peeled and sliced in rings* | 5 |
| 2 Tablespoons | olive oil | 30 mL |
| 2 Tablespoons | tomato paste | 30 mL |
| 3/4 teaspoon | garlic powder | 3 mL |
| pinch | white pepper | pinch |
| pinch | cayenne | pinch |
| 1 teaspoon | sugar | 5 mL |
| 1 Tablespoon | maple syrup | 15 mL |

- To boiling water in stockpot add chicken soup base, reduce heat, simmer for 2 minutes.
- In a separate pan, fry onions in olive oil for 7-10 minutes – or until cooked and lightly browned. Add onions to chicken soup base. Add balance of ingredients. Return to boil, reduce heat, cover, simmer for 15 minutes.
- Taste for salt – need for salt depends on brand of soup base used.
- Serves 8

## Mulligatawny

| | | |
|---|---|---|
| 1 | onion, *peeled and chopped* | 1 |
| 1 | leek, *chopped* | 1 |
| 1 large | carrot, *peeled and grated* | 1 large |
| 2 Tablespoons | olive oil | 30 mL |
| 2 Tablespoons | potato flour | 30 mL |
| 2 teaspoons | hot curry powder | 10 mL |
| 1 teaspoon | salt | 5 mL |
| 5 cups | chicken stock *(see page 114)* | 1.2 L |
| 2 1/2 cups | water | 625 mL |
| 1 cup | chopped mushrooms | 250 mL |
| 3/4 cup | chopped cooked chicken | 175 mL |
| 2 cups | cooked basmati rice | 500 mL |

- Fry onion, leek, carrot in olive oil for 2 minutes. Add potato flour, curry powder, salt and continue to cook for another 2 minutes.
- Add chicken stock and water, bring to boil, reduce heat, cover, simmer for 15 minutes.
- Add mushrooms, chicken, cooked rice and continue to simmer for 5 minutes.
- **Serves 6**  *(Picture on front cover)*

*This is a fun soup with the hot curry powder and the rice and mushrooms and chicken. Try it if you haven't tried hot curry powder – it is not too hot.*

THE GRACIOUS TABLE: SOUPS BY CAROL

1. Parsnip Vegetable Soup
2. Turkey Soup
3. Parsnip Apple Soup
4. Sweet and Sour Pork Soup

100 / Vegetable Soups with Meat

## Parsnip Vegetable Soup

| 7 1/2 cups | water | 1.7 L |
| --- | --- | --- |
| 3 Tablespoons | gluten free chicken soup base | 45 mL |
| 2 | carrots, *peeled and sliced* | 2 |
| 2 | potatoes, *peeled and sliced* | 2 |
| 2 | onions, *peeled and sliced* | 2 |
| 3 | apples, *peeled and sliced* | 3 |
| 4 | parsnips, *peeled and sliced* | 4 |
| 1 teaspoon | dried basil leaves | 5 mL |
| 1/2 teaspoon | dried mint leaves | 2 mL |
| pinch | cayenne | pinch |

- Bring water to boil in large stockpot, add chicken soup base, stir. Add vegetables and apples, bring to boil, reduce heat, simmer covered for 30 minutes. Blend with hand blender. Add seasonings, stir and serve.
- Serves 6

## Turkey Soup

| 4 cups | turkey stock *(see page 114)* | 1 L |
| --- | --- | --- |
| 2 cups | water | 500 mL |
| 1/4 cup | uncooked brown rice | 60 mL |
| 2 cups | frozen mixed vegetables | 500 mL |
| 3/4 cup | cooked turkey, *diced* | 175 mL |
| 1 clove | garlic, *peeled and crushed* | 1 clove |
| 1/2 teaspoon | salt | 2 mL |
| 1/8 teaspoon | white pepper | 0.5 mL |

- Place in stockpot: turkey stock, water and rice. Bring to boil, reduce heat, cover, simmer for 25 minutes.
- Add remainder of ingredients, continue to simmer for 5 minutes.
- Serves 6

## Parsnip Apple Soup

| 8 cups | water | 1.8 L |
|---|---|---|
| 3 Tablespoons | gluten free chicken soup base | 45 mL |
| 2 1/2 cups | parsnips, *peeled and chopped* | 625 mL |
| 1 cup | chopped celery, *strings removed* | 250 mL |
| 2 Tablespoons | olive oil | 30 mL |
| 1 large | onion, *peeled and chopped* | 1 large |
| 1 medium | red pepper, *peeled and chopped* | 1 medium |
| 3 | apples, *peeled and chopped* | 3 |
| 3 Tablespoons | tapioca starch | 45 mL |
| 1 teaspoon | dried marjoram leaves | 5 mL |
| pinch | cayenne | pinch |
| 1 Tablespoon | maple syrup | 15 mL |

- In large stockpot stir chicken soup base into boiling water, simmer for 3 minutes. Add parsnips and celery, continue to simmer for 15 minutes. Set aside.

- In large saucepan place: olive oil, onion, red pepper, apples. Stir over medium heat for 5 minutes, stir in tapioca flour and continue to cook for 5 minutes.

- Add onion-red pepper-apple mixture to soup mixture in large stockpot. Add marjoram, cayenne, maple syrup. Bring to boil, reduce heat, cover, simmer for 5 minutes. Blend with hand blender. Taste for salt.

- Serves 6-8

## Sweet and Sour Pork Soup

| | | |
|---|---|---|
| 1 lb | pork side ribs, *cut in small pieces* | 500 g |
| 8 cups | water | 1.8 L |
| 2 Tablespoons | apple cider vinegar | 30 mL |
| 1 teaspoon | salt | 5 mL |
| 3 | bay leaves | 3 |
| 1 | onion, *peeled and chopped* | 1 |
| 1/2 small | cabbage, *peeled and grated* | 1/2 small |
| 1/2 | red pepper, *peeled and diced* | 1/2 |
| 1/3 bulb | fennel, *trimmed and diced* | 1/3 bulb |
| 2 | apples, *peeled and diced* | 2 |
| 1 teaspoon | dried thyme | 5 mL |
| pinch | cayenne | pinch |
| 1 Tablespoon | sugar | 15 mL |
| 2 cups | water | 454 mL |

- Place pork side ribs in water, add apple cider vinegar, salt, bay leaves, chopped onion. Bring to boil, reduce heat, cover, simmer for 2 hours.
- Strain soup into large bowl, discard 3 bay leaves, onion, pork bones – reserving meat to add to soup. This straining will yield 5 cups (1.2 L) pork stock.
- To lift fat off top of stock, place a paper towel on the top of the stock and lift off quickly. Repeat this 4-5 times. - OR - Cover stock and place in refrigerator for several hours until fat settles to the top, then lift off and proceed with recipe.
- Return pork stock and reserved, chopped meat to stockpot. Add all other ingredients. Return to boil, reduce heat, cover, simmer for 30 minutes.
- Serves 6

THE GRACIOUS TABLE: SOUPS BY CAROL

1 Lemon Vegetable Soup
2 Blended Vegetable Soup
3 Vegetable Beef Soup
4 Tart Vegetable Soup

## LEMON VEGETABLE SOUP

### FIRST STEP – CHICKEN STOCK

*N.B. Be sure that any sauce used in cooking the chicken is gluten free.*

| | | |
|---|---|---|
| skin & bones only of | 1 cooked chicken | skin & bones only |
| 2 | onions, *peeled and chopped* | 2 |
| 2 | carrots, *peeled and sliced* | 2 |
| 4 | bay leaves | 4 |
| 1 teaspoon | salt | 5 mL |
| 10 cups | water | 2.2 L |

- Place all of the above in a stockpot, bring to the boil, reduce heat, cover and simmer for 2 hours. Strain, reserve stock (liquid) – it will yield 8 cups (1.8 L). Discard bones, skin, 4 bay leaves, onions and carrots.

### SECOND STEP – SOUP

| | | |
|---|---|---|
| 2 large | potatoes, *peeled and chopped* | 2 large |
| 5 | carrots, *peeled and chopped* | 5 |
| 2 | apples, *peeled and chopped* | 2 |
| juice of 1 | lemon | juice of 1 |
| 1 | zucchini, *peeled and sliced* | 1 |
| 2 cups | water | 500 mL |
| 1/8 teaspoon | garlic powder | 0.5 mL |
| 1/8 teaspoon | white pepper | 0.5 mL |
| 1 teaspoon | celery salt | 5 mL |
| 1 teaspoon | dried basil | 5 mL |
| 1/4 teaspoon | salt | 1 mL |
| 2 teaspoons | sugar | 10 mL |

- Add all soup ingredients to the reserved chicken stock in large stockpot. Bring to the boil, reduce heat, cover, simmer for 30 minutes. Blend with hand blender.
- Serves 6-8

## Blended Vegetable Soup

| | | |
|---|---|---|
| 7 cups | water | 1.6 mL |
| 2 Tablespoons | gluten free chicken soup base | 30 mL |
| 3 medium | zucchini, *peeled and sliced* | 3 medium |
| 4 | carrots, *peeled and sliced* | 4 |
| 2 | potatoes, *peeled and sliced* | 2 |
| 2 | onions, *peeled and chopped* | 2 |
| 3 | apples, *peeled and sliced* | 3 |
| 2 | celery stocks | 2 |
| 1 | tomato, *skinned and chopped* | 1 |
| 1/2 cup | orange juice | 125 mL |
| 1 teaspoon | dried basil | 5 mL |
| 1 teaspoon | dried dill weed | 5 mL |
| 3/4 teaspoon | dried ginger | 3 mL |
| 1/8 teaspoon | black pepper | 0.5 mL |
| 1/4 teaspoon | cinnamon | 1 mL |
| 2 cloves | garlic, *chopped* | 2 cloves |

- Place gluten free chicken soup base in boiling water, stir and simmer for 3 minutes, then add all ingredients in large stockpot, bring to boil, reduce heat, cover, simmer for 25 minutes or until all vegetables are cooked.
- Blend with hand blender.
- Taste for salt. Add if required.
- Serves 6

*This is a lot of vegetables, but once prepared, the cooking is quick – then to blend – and to enjoy.*

## VEGETABLE BEEF

| | | |
|---|---|---|
| 3 quarts | water | 2.7 L |
| 1 lb | lean minced beef | 500 g |
| 1 large | onion, *peeled and chopped* | 1 large |
| 5 | bay leaves | 5 |
| 1 1/2 teaspoons | salt | 7 mL |
| 4 | carrots, *peeled and sliced* | 4 |
| 28 oz | tin ground tomatoes | 796 mL |
| 1 cup | gluten free small pasta | 250 mL |
| 1 cup | frozen peas | 250 mL |
| 2 Tablespoons | sugar | 30 mL |
| pinch | white pepper | pinch |

- Bring water to boil in stockpot. Add minced beef, onion, bay leaves, salt, carrots, tomatoes. Return to boil, reduce heat, cover, simmer for 30 minutes.
- Add pasta, peas, sugar and pepper. Return to boil, reduce heat, cover, simmer for 15 minutes.
- Remove 5 bay leaves before serving.
- Serves 12

*This is a variation of vegetable soup with tomatoes, pasta and beef. Try a few vegetable soups to see which you prefer.*

## Tart Vegetable Soup

| | | |
|---|---|---|
| 6 cups | boiling water | 1.4 L |
| 4 Tablespoons | gluten free chicken soup base | 60 mL |
| 3 | carrots, *peeled and thinly sliced* | 3 |
| 1 | onion, *peeled and chopped* | 1 |
| 1 small | zucchini, *peeled and diced* | 1 small |
| 1 | cucumber, *peeled, seeds removed, diced* | 1 |
| 2 | tomatoes, *peeled and chopped* | 2 |
| 1 cup | broccoli, *flowerets with short stem* | 250 mL |
| 3/4 cup | tinned ground tomatoes | 175 mL |
| 1/2 | green pepper, *peeled and diced* | 1/2 |
| 1/2 teaspoon | celery salt | 2 mL |
| 1/2 teaspoon | dried dill weed | 2 mL |
| pinch | white pepper | pinch |
| 1 Tablespoon | sugar | 15 mL |

- To 6 cups (1.4 L) boiling water, add chicken soup base, stir, simmer for 3 minutes.
- Add carrots and onion, return to boil, reduce heat, cover, simmer for 15 minutes. Add all other ingredients, bring to boil, reduce heat, cover, simmer for 7 minutes.
- Serves 6-7

*What makes it tart? The tomatoes and the combination of all ingredients and very little sugar.*

# Soup Stock

*FISH STOCK*
*BEEF STOCK*
*PORK STOCK*
*LAMB STOCK*
*(4 pictures, page 110)*

*TURKEY STOCK*
*CHICKEN STOCK*
*VEGETABLE STOCK*
*(3 pictures, page 113)*

THE GRACIOUS TABLE: SOUPS BY CAROL

1 Fish Stock
2 Beef Stock
3 Pork Stock
4 Lamb Stock

## Fish Stock

| | | |
|---|---|---|
| 1 pound | halibut & doré, *bones, skin and flesh* | 500 g |
| 4 1/2 cups | water | 1 L |
| 2 | bay leaves | 2 |
| 1/2 teaspoon | salt | 2 mL |
| 1 | onion, *peeled and chopped* | 1 |
| 2 | carrots, *peeled and sliced* | 2 |

- Place fish bones, skin, flesh, water, bay leaves, salt, onion and carrots in stockpot.
- Bring to boil, reduce heat, cover and simmer for 25 minutes.
- Strain, reserving stock. Discard 2 bay leaves, carrots, skin and bones. Carefully feel fish for bones and set aside flesh for fish chowder or eat with gluten free crackers.
- Yields 3 cups (750 mL) fish stock.

## Beef Stock

| | | |
|---|---|---|
| several | bones & gristle from beef roast | several |
| 6 cups | water | 1.4 L |
| 1 | onion, *chopped* | 1 |
| 4 stalks | celery, *chopped* | 4 stalks |
| 2 | bay leaves | 2 |
| 1 Tablespoon | apple cider vinegar | 15 mL |
| 1/2 teaspoon | salt | 2 mL |

- Place all ingredients in stockpot, bring to boil, reduce heat, cover and simmer for 2 hours.
- Strain, reserving stock; discard bones, gristle and 2 bay leaves; cover stock and refrigerate for several hours or overnight. Lift fat off top and discard.
- Yields 3 cups (750 mL) beef stock.

## Pork Stock

| 3 pounds | pork spare ribs, *cut in pieces* | 1.5 kg |
| 12 cups | water | 2.7 L |
| 2 | bay leaves | 2 |
| 1 teaspoon | salt | 5 mL |

- Place all ingredients in large stockpot, bring to boil; reduce heat, cover and simmer for 2 1/2 hours.
- Remove and discard 2 bay leaves. Strain stock into large bowl, cool, cover with plastic wrap, refrigerate overnight.
- Next day, lift fat off the top, pour stock into plastic containers. Refrigerate or freeze for future use.
- Yields 8 cups (1.8 L) pork stock.

## Lamb Stock

| lamb bone | from leg or other parts of lamb | lamb bone |
| 8 cups | water | 1.8 L |
| 3 | bay leaves | 3 |
| 1 Tablespoon | apple cider vinegar | 15 mL |
| 1 teaspoon | salt | 5 mL |

- Place all ingredients in stockpot, bring to boil; reduce heat, cover and simmer for 2 hours.
- Remove bones and 3 bay leaves; strain, cool, cover and refrigerate overnight.
- In the morning lift fat off top and discard it.
- Yields 6 cups (1.4 L) lamb stock.

*100 Gluten Free Soups*

1 Turkey Stock
2 Chicken Stock
3 Vegetable Stock

Soup Stock / 113

## Turkey Stock

| | | |
|---|---|---|
| several | bones from turkey breast | several |
| 8 cups | water | 1.8 L |
| 1/2 teaspoon | salt | 2 mL |
| 2 | bay leaves | 2 |
| 1 | onion, *peeled and chopped* | 1 |
| 2 | carrots, *peeled and chopped* | 2 |
| 2 stalks | celery, *chopped* | 2 stalks |
| 1 Tablespoon | apple cider vinegar | 15 mL |

- Place all ingredients in stockpot, bring to boil, reduce heat, cover and simmer for 2 hours.
- Strain reserving stock, discard bones and 2 bay leaves, reserve any meat from bones for soup, cover the stock, refrigerate for several hours or overnight. Lift fat off top and discard.
- Yields 4 cups (1 L) turkey stock.

## Chicken Stock

| | | |
|---|---|---|
| 1 BBQ chicken | bones and skin only | 1 BBQ chicken |
| 1 | onion, *peeled and chopped* | 1 |
| 9 cups | water | 2 L |
| 1/2 teaspoon | salt | 2 mL |

*(Note: Be sure the BBQ chicken sauce used on the chicken skin is gluten free.)*

- Place all of the above in stockpot, bring to boil, reduce heat, cover and simmer for 2 hours.
- Pass soup through a strainer, discard bones and skin.
- Place stock in bowl in refrigerator overnight to let fat rise to the top. Lift fat off the top next morning and discard.
- Yields 5 cups (1.2 L) chicken stock.

## VEGETABLE STOCK

| | | |
|---|---|---|
| 8 | **onions,** *peeled and cut in quarters* | 8 |
| 3 tablespoons | olive oil | 45 mL |
| 9 | **carrots,** *peeled and cut in large pieces* | 9 |
| 3 stalks | **celery,** *cut in large pieces* | 3 stalks |
| 6 3/4 quarts | cold water | 6 L |
| 1 1/4 teaspoons | salt | 6 mL |
| 28 oz | tin ground tomatoes | 796 mL |
| 5 1/2 oz | tin tomato paste | 156 mL |

- Brown onions in olive oil. Place all ingredients in large stockpot. Bring to boil, reduce heat, cover and simmer for 2 hours.
- Remove from heat, strain and reserve stock for Onion Soup and Pepperpot Soup. Vegetables can be used in Pepperpot Soup.
- Cool the vegetables and blend in food processor.
- Blended vegetables and soup stock both freeze well – but freeze them separately for separate use.
- Yields 6 3/4 quarts (6 L) of stock and 9 cups (2 L) of blended vegetables.

*These stocks – meat, fish, vegetable – are the bases of many soups – though not of all. They can be frozen in different size containers and used when needed. They do enrich a recipe.*

# INDEX

**A**

apple
  cinnamon, 3
  zucchini, 85

**B**

banana, 3
beef stock, 111
blended
  green lentil, 56
  lentil, 52
  vegetable, 106
borscht, 4
broccoli
  chicken, 90
  ginger, 36
  parsley, 70
brussel sprouts, 38

**C**

carrot
  cabbage, 85
  cucumber, 69
  curried, 38
  ginger, 71
  orange, 72
  spicy, 86
celery
  chicken, 88
  ginger, 19
  onion, 20
  tarragon, 19
  tomato, 89
chick pea, 64
chicken
  broccoli, 90
  noodle, 92
  stock, 114
  zucchini, 92

chilled
  avocado, 12
  banana, 3
  borscht, 4
  cantaloupe, 10
  cinnamon, 3
  cucumber, 8
  pea, 12
  peach, 7
  pineapple, 10
  sour cherry, 5
  strawberry, 5
  sweet medley, 13
  sweet mystery, 9
  turnip, 7
chowder
  clam, 42
  corn, 22
  halibut, 45
  Montreal, 46
  scallop, 42
  seafood, 41
  shrimp, 44
  turbot, 41
cream of
  asparagus, 17
  cauliflower, 18
  corn, 22
  mushroom, 24
  rutabaga, 35
  tomato, 32
  turnip, 7
creamy green veg, 31
cucumber
  carrot, 69
  chilled, 8
curried carrot, 38

**F**

fish stock, 111
four bean, 59
french onion, 75

**G**

gazpacho
  chilled, 13
  warm, 93
ginger
  broccoli, 36
  carrot, 71
  cherry, 89
  squash, 27
  strawberry, 29
  vegetable, 78
green, 71
  lentil, 51
  split pea, 56

**H**

halibut chowder, 45
hearty vegetable, 80

**L**

lamb stock, 112
leek
  parsnip, 93
  potato, 23
lemon
  cheddar, 95
  vegetable, 105
lentil, 49
  blended, 52
  blended green, 56
  green, 51
  green split pea, 56
  red, 50
  vegetarian, 50

# INDEX

## M
minestrone, 97
Montreal chowder, 46
mulligatawny, 99
multi-vegetable, 63
mushroom, 24

## O
old bones, 96
onion, 75
    French, 75
    for 8, 98
orange
    carrot, 72
    turnip, 73

## P
parsnip
    apple, 102
    mint, 77
    vegetable, 101
pea with mint, 12
peach, 7
pepperpot, 81
pineapple, 10
pork stock, 112
potato & leek, 23
pumpkin, 26

## Q
quick & chunky, 62

## R
red lentil, 50
rutabaga, 35

## S
scallop chowder, 42
seafood delight, 41
shrimp bisque, 44
six bean, 60
sour cherry, 5
spaghetti squash, 65
spicy carrot, 86
spinach, 37
squash
    chick pea, 62
    ginger, 27
stock
    beef, 111
    chicken, 114
    fish, 111
    lamb, 112
    pork, 112
    turkey, 114
    vegetable, 115
strawberry
    chilled, 5
    ginger, 29
    vegetable, 80
sweet
    medley, 13
    mystery, 9
    potato, 28
sweet and sour, 103

## T
tart vegetable, 108
tomato
    celery, 89
    cream of, 32
    rice, 77
    vegetable, 82
turbot chowder, 41
turkey, 101
turkey stock, 114
turnip
    chilled, 7
    orange, 73

## V
vegetable
    beef, 107
    blended creamy green, 31
    ginger, 78
    hearty, 80
    lemon, 105
    parsnip, 101
    stock, 115
    strawberry, 80
    tart, 108
    tomato, 82
vegetarian, 50
vichyssoise, 23

## W
warm gazpacho, 93
watercress, 32
white kidney beans, 60

## Y
yellow
    split pea, 54
    & green split pea, 57

## Z
zucchini
    apple, 85
    bean, 59
    chicken, 92

## About the Author

Carol Tansey believes that food is terribly important for health and that it is just as easy to make that food delicious – as not.

Carol studied Nutrition at Macdonald College of McGill University, as well as having a life-long interest in research in many areas pertaining to food. She also has a Certificate in Management in Health and Social Services from McGill University.

Carol's experience covers – Strawberry Festivals for 200, Buffet Suppers, Country Luncheons, Anniversary Parties, Funeral Receptions, Formal Dinners, Birthday Parties, Afternoon Tea Parties, Bake Sales, and Cooking Contests – Province-wide, where she won several awards.

Books by Carol Tansey:   The Gracious Table – Desserts by Carol

The Gracious Table – Soups by Carol
*100 Gluten Free Soups*

www.ingramcontent.com/pod-product-compliance
Lightning Source LLC
Chambersburg PA
CBHW041958150426
43194CB00002B/56